I Said Yes!

**REAL LIFE STORIES OF STUDENTS, TEACHERS AND LEADERS
SAYING *YES!* TO YOUTH ENTREPRENEURSHIP
IN AMERICA'S SCHOOLS**

JULIE SILARD KANTOR

Gazelles
GROWING LEADERS, GROWING COMPANIES

First printing

*For privacy, some names and minor details have been changed in this book.

ISBN-10: 0-9765823-6-8,
ISBN-13: 978-0-9765823-6-6
PUBLISHED BY GAZELLES, INC.
www. Gazelles.com
Virginia

Printed in the United States of America

This book is dedicated to all the NFTE teachers and businesspeople out there who are on the front lines saying Yes! and taking action to bring the life skill of entrepreneurship to high school classrooms across America and abroad.

With deep appreciation to the greatest teacher and social entrepreneur who, through his dream, laid a foundation for so many of us to DREAM and BUILD, Steve Mariotti, NFTE's founder, and to Mike Caslin, my friend and NFTE's CEO for believing in me before I believed in myself.

To my family — thanks for teaching me to "walk" to "sing" to "love" to "question" and to "dream."

Acknowledgments:

Special thanks to so many who have SAID YES! with me:

My husband, Marc, for his endless love, guidance, and support. To my daughter Justine, for teaching me to live in the present moment and to love with all my heart. My brother Tony, for being a source of inspiration and for his personal and professional coaching. My mother Joan, for her optimism, love, and positive mirroring. My father Steve, for teaching me about the American Dream through the example of his life and giving me courage and inner strength. My step-parents, Monique and Mario, for being great role models for love, family, and marriage. My in-laws, Carole and Mel, for their unconditional love. My siblings: Danny, Andrew, Zena, and Perry — family is the foundation — always!

To Steve Mariotti, Mike Caslin, David Nelson and the employees and fellow social entrepreneurs at NFTE. I also need to spotlight the self-described "Divas" of NFTE Greater Washington, who have gone above and beyond to help build the program: Verice White (my partner for five years), Jackie French, Janet Lau, Dalissa Vargas, Kate Burns, and Tricia Granata. Our teachers are on the front lines and the "heart" of NFTE-GW. I'd like to acknowledge all our teachers, and in particular thank Mena Lofland, Tom Brown, Sereta Coleman, Dale Lubkeman, Valarie Wheeler, Rene Meddaugh, Mary Sturdivant, Marilyn Hollis, Cherel Fitzgerald, Aloha Cobb, and Derek Sontz for setting the benchmark and going above and beyond.

I Said Yes! happened as a result of some of the best minds and advisors a woman could ask for. Some of the top entrepreneurial leaders in the region have devoted their time and effort in the service of NFTE's mission, and I am forever indebted to them: Patty Alper, S. Tien Wong, Brien Biondi, David Roodberg, Larry and Jan Rivitz, Phil McNeill, Bill Walton, James Kimsey, Joe Robert, Charlene Drew Jarvis, Edie Fraser, Leonard James, Sandy Butler Wyte, Maxine Baker, Kathleen Zeifang, David Koch, Liz Koch, Arthur Dade, Anne Allen, Sidney Smith, Bob Corlett, Michelle Courton Brown, Kathy Korman Frey, Cathy Lange, Mary MacPherson, Mario Morino, Julia Spicer, Marie Johns, Diana Davis Spencer, Abby and Nat Moffat, Donn Weinberg, Brian Merritt, Jasper Wilson, Steve Tarason, DC Public School's Office of Career and Technology Education, Elaine Romanelli, Larry Robertson, Lucas Ames, Lindsley Lowell, Minal Damani, Teri Galvez, Paul Wisenthal, and the NFTE Adopt-a-Class Pioneers.

This book would not have happened without the encouragement of Verne Harnish, my Publisher and President of Gazelles Inc., and my two outstanding editors, Gideon Berger and Tony Towle.

BACKGROUND

Founded in 1987 by Steve Mariotti (a former business executive and entrepreneur) while he was a public high school teacher in New York City's South Bronx, NFTE began as a program to prevent dropout and improve academic performance among students who were at risk of failing or quitting school. Combining his business background with his desire to teach at-risk students, Steve discovered that when low-income youth are given the opportunity to learn about entrepreneurship, their innate "street smarts" can easily develop into "academic smarts" and "business smarts." Through entrepreneurship, youth discover that what they are learning in the classroom is relevant to the real world.

NFTE is widely viewed as a world leader in promoting entrepreneurial literacy among youth. When young people participate in our programs they begin to unlock their unique entrepreneurial creativity, have a greater understanding of the free enterprise system, improve the quality of their lives, and dare to dream for bright futures.

To date, NFTE has worked with over 140,000 young people from low-income communities from 35 States across the U.S. and in fourteen countries around the world.

Foreword: The Challenge and the Hope

By Steve Mariotti, Founder and President,
The National Foundation for Teaching Entrepreneurship (NFTE)

I have discovered something that — if fully understood by our government, business, and community leaders — could have enormously positive implications for the future of our society. Simply put, it is this: Children born into poverty have special gifts that prepare them for business formation and wealth creation. They are mentally strong, resilient, and full of chutzpah. They are skeptical of hierarchies and the status quo. They are long-suffering in the face of adversity. They are comfortable with risk and uncertainty. They know how to deal with stress and conflict.

Perhaps, ironically, these attitudes and abilities make these children ideally suited for breaking out of the cycle of dependency that so often comes with poverty, and for getting ahead in the marketplace. In short, poor kids are "street smart," which transforms into "business smart" when channeled in the right direction. Precisely because of their experience surviving in a challenging world, they are able to perceive and pursue fleeting opportunities that others, more content with their lot in life, tend to miss.

More often than not, the statistics we read about poverty, broken families, lack of educational opportunity, low performance in schools, and juvenile crime can fill us with frustration and a sense of hopelessness. Progress on these issues over the last several decades has been modest to say the least, despite a myriad of government programs costing billions of dollars, along with the heroic efforts of countless administrators, teachers, volunteers, and children and their families who are trying to change their lives for the better. This book, *I Said Yes!*, written by my good friend and colleague of 15 years, Julie Silard Kantor, offers great hope for getting children who are highly at risk out of this cycle of dependency and despondency — for good.

We at NFTE believe that entrepreneurship can be a vital connector between at-risk kids and their schools, their communities, and the workplace, and can inspire and empower them to build a vision for the future. Since NFTE's inception, we have reached over 140,000 such children, trained more than 4,000 Certified Entrepreneurship Teachers, and continually developed and improved our innovative entrepreneurship curriculum.

Despite our success, NFTE's work is needed more urgently today than ever before, with more American children living in poverty and their parents having more difficulty finding work. According to reports by the Annie E. Casey Foundation and the Federal Interagency Forum on Child and Family Statistics, nearly 13 million American children (18%) were living in poverty in 2004. The family also continues to break down. Some 31% of American children lived in a single-parent household in 2004, a 23% increase from 1980. One-third lived in a household where neither parent had a full-time job, a 3% increase from 2001. Only 51% of all black students and 52% of all Hispanic students graduate from high school according to the Manhattan Institute, and only 20% of all black students and 16% of all Hispanic students leave high school college-ready. And, perhaps most disquieting, serious violent crime among our young people has risen sharply, to 18 per 1,000 in 2003, from 10 per 1,000 the previous year.

These statistics aren't just indicators of social problems in our society. They demonstrate that America's future economic competitiveness is at stake. NFTE inspires at-risk kids to stay in high school (and to go on to college) by awakening an interest in business, showing them a viable path to economic independence and, along the way, making positive life-choices and participating in the larger society.

Research on NFTE's impact conducted by the Harvard School of Education demonstrates that at-risk children who receive entrepreneurship training have a stronger desire to seek higher education, do more independent reading, and — perhaps most importantly — feel more connected to their schools and communities and more in control of their lives and the future. Whether these young people ultimately decide to work for themselves or someone else is irrelevant. What they gain from learning entrepreneurship is a fundamental life skill that can impact their sense of well-being and locus of control.

I Said Yes! will introduce you to the growing movement to teach entrepreneurship to young people from low-income communities. Julie Silard Kantor — a 2005 winner of NFTE's Leadership Award and former NFTE Executive of the Year — has built in our nation's capital what is widely recognized as one of the top youth entrepreneurship programs in the country. *I Said Yes!* is Julie's first-person account of the transformative power that NFTE's mission of teaching entrepreneurship has brought to so many young lives — including her own. It is both the story of Julie's path into youth development and teaching, and of the many troubled youths who overcame significant obstacles to make their lives productive and meaningful.

Today, we are confident that our program is adding significant value to thousands of young people's lives. By combining the most recent technology with the time-tested principles of free enterprise, we are developing solutions for one of the most serious threats to our society—poverty. We are continuing our efforts to go to scale and create a national movement in which every low-income child is taught entrepreneurial skills and elementary business principles.

Our vision is that, by the year 2012, Title I Schools in the United States and cities around the world will offer an entrepreneurship course as an elective — or, ideally, as a foundation course as part of an Academy structure, that is, specialty schools operating within one building. We hope to expand NFTE to the 30 largest U.S. cities and work closely with superintendents and educators who are ready to say *yes* to a proven and timely program model. This is a curriculum that will meet the challenge and assist young people in becoming economically productive members of society.

We are fortunate to have dedicated men and women, like Julie, who are striving to accomplish our mission. But an equally valuable asset is the unquenchable optimism of the youth we serve. As one of our graduates so aptly put it, "My dream is not to die in poverty, but to have poverty die in me."

I Said *Yes!*

YOUTH ENTREPRENEURSHIP

T A B L E   O F   C O N T E N T S

Deshaun Houston And The American Dream

Deshaun's 6-foot, 300-pound frame towered over my 5 foot 6 inches. His lower lip twitched as he stared down at me. He was about to cry! Was he mad at me or mad at life? I wondered.

"It's not that I don't care, Ms. Julie," he said, "it's that I *can't do math*!"

It was the summer of 1993 in Brockton, Massachusetts, on a particularly hot and sticky day. The shoe manufacturing capital of the world in the early 1900s, Brockton was now strewn with abandoned hulks of factories, and other grim reminders on the desolate streets, of a once-vibrant economy. A few remaining downtown storefronts displayed "Going Out of Business" signs. Deshaun and other residents were subject to periodic "brown-outs," and sometimes there was no electricity at all. Now it seemed that a recent graduate from Brockton High had never really learned to add or subtract. I wondered how Deshaun had made it through school.

Even with a high school diploma, Deshaun's future seemed uncertain and bleak. Eighteen years old, raised by a single mother who was living on public assistance, Deshaun felt the pressure of being the man of the house and the need to help raise his four younger siblings. Several months before joining my class, a stray bullet had torn straight through Deshaun's calf while he was at a party. He told me he had "been in the wrong place at the wrong time."

But rather than dwell on the negatives in his life, Deshaun had come up with inventive solutions. One was for a refrigerator with a backup battery that would provide power during the brown-outs that often spoiled his family's and neighbors' groceries. Another was for a convenience store on wheels, to provide goods no longer available in town, to bring ordinary consumer items to those unwilling to risk Brockton's dangerous streets.

At this summer BizCamp I was teaching at the Boys and Girls Clubs of Brockton for the National Foundation for Teaching Entrepreneurship (NFTE) — a "mini-MBA" program for low-income youth — Deshaun finally seemed to be in the right place at the right time. With his innate charm and sparkling brown eyes, Deshaun soon became the class leader and chief motivator — as well as my favorite student. He shared his ideas about how he could improve people's lives in his hometown while satisfying their needs as consumers. "I'd be like the ice cream man but with more products," he told the class. "A lot of people are scared to go out at night, so the Deshaun's Convenience Store on Wheels van would come around, and I'd be sellin' VCR tapes, baby formula, diapers — whatever they'd need."

On this particular afternoon, I was setting up a lesson on the concept of Return on Investment: "Let's say that one day your brother invests $2 so you can start a lemonade business," I had begun. "Then, at the end of the day, you have sold $5 worth of

2

lemonade. So you give your brother back the loan plus $2, or $4 total. What was the return on his investment?" (The formula is: what you made [$4 − $2 = $2] over what you paid [$2 at the beginning of the day] times 100 (4 − 2 over 2 = 1 times 100 = 100%). Exercises such as these were an integral part of the NFTE course as set out in its textbook, *How to Start and Operate a Small Business.* As I asked each student to take a turn answering these kind of simple math questions, I noticed Deshaun closing his book and avoiding eye contact. He leaned back in his seat with his arms folded.

"Deshaun, you're next," I said.

He looked away.

"Deshaun?"

His eyes met mine. Suddenly his defiance turned into an empty gaze, as he stared at the floor.

"Deshaun, would you like to do the next one? Number 8, I believe, on page 86?"

"Nope," he finally replied.

"Deshaun, can you open your book to page 86?"

"Don't care to."

Now, this is a real tough moment for a teacher. My top student was basically telling me to "F-off." Deshaun looked both defeated and irritated with me. I didn't know what to do.

"Deshaun, can I see you outside, please?" I asked, and had my teacher's assistant take over the class. I tried not to embarrass students in front of their peers.

"Deshaun, you have been the best student in this class, and the others all look up to you," I said, remembering to start with a positive comment before stating my concern. "When you say that you "don't care to," what message does that send to everyone else?"

Keeping my poise, and with a very stern face, I then said, "Deshaun, can you please tell me what is going on here? I can't let you ruin the class today."

"I can't do the math, Ms. Julie," he said plaintively.

"OK, Deshaun, if I give you a dollar," and I handed him one, "and at the end of the day you give me back two, after you made five dollars selling lemonade, how much is what you give back to me compared to what you started with?"

In one hand, like a scale, Deshaun held the dollar I gave him, and in the other he held an imaginary dollar that he was going to give me.

"It's the same," he said. "I'll give you back the same amount that you gave me plus another dollar."

"So is it 100% of what you started with?"

"Yes," he said.

"Another question, Deshaun. When we went to New York

and you bought those 'music star' T-shirts for $36 a dozen many did you get?"

"I bought 12 shirts, Ms. Julie. They cost me $3 each."

"How many did you sell?"

He replied, with a big smile, that he had sold eight for $10 each.

"So how much did you make when we were selling our products at the Unity Festival?"

"Eighty dollars — no, ninety, 'cause I sold the Janet Jackson one to my aunt later on that weekend."

I saw recognition light up in Deshaun's face. Earlier, he had shared his great sales results with the class, and I knew this was a source of pride.

"So, how much did you spend on those nine?"

Deshaun started counting on his fingers. His lips moved as he counted; he got frustrated and counted again.

"Twenty-six — no, 27 dollars," he said proudly.

"Deshaun, I don't know if you realize this, but you are doing math, my friend! Let's go back into class now and we can work more on all this. I want you to be really strong and confident in business."

This moment freed Deshaun from his paralysis of not know-

classroom. He went on to sell many more shirts rning more than $500 each month. At the same sense of outrage passed through me. How could h so much potential and passion graduate from he belief that he could not do simple math prob- Deshaun slip through the cracks of our educational system? What would his future hold if he didn't have the basics? Deshaun, as with millions of other economically disadvantaged youths , would be prevented from working in the business world and pursuing entrepreneurship simply because they could not read and write or do simple math. How can we ensure that students are prepared to make it both in the market economy and as good citizens? How would Deshaun make it?

That day showed me that many young people do not have the confidence they need in the ability to perform basic but crucial career-related tasks — whether math, reading, writing, or speaking in public. But I've seen this lack of confidence shift in young people time and again when it comes to showing them how to make money through their own businesses.

The *I can't* suddenly becomes *I can*, when math and reading are shown to have practical, real-life applications. Something as simple as getting business cards made or filling in an inventory or sales sheet can spark the inspiration to figure out math, create flyers, check spelling, learn to use a computer, and speak to strangers, as they relate to building a small business and getting customers to buy their products. I often tell my students: "The last four letters in *American* are *I can*." With appropriate training, education, start-up capital, and access to the resources of our market economy, young people *can* be economically productive members of society and lead fulfilling lives.

Earl Tate is an example of what can happen when people choose to take control of their lives despite initial disadvantages. Having grown up in poverty in a tough neighborhood in Louisiana, Earl became one of my first board members when I was the director of NFTE's Boston (later, New England) operations. He spoke to Deshaun's class that summer and at one point pulled up his sleeve and showed two scars, where he had had gang tattoos removed. "Out of nine friends I had growing up, eight are now dead or in jail," Earl said. He told the class that he had been lucky to have escaped a life of gangs and street fights, which would have led to prison and perhaps death. Deshaun had edged forward in his seat, listening intently, soaking up every word.

Earl talked about running across a copy of *Better Homes and Gardens*. He asked himself why he couldn't live as well as the people in the magazine. "I decided to make a change in my life," he told the class. He started a small business in high school, typing term papers for other students, charging a few dollars a page. After a few months, he decided he truly hated typing, so he hired other people to do the work, and then marketed the business for a 50% cut of the revenues.

Earl would eventually found one of the largest minority-owned temporary staffing agencies in the country. While he was growing up, Earl's mother worked as a maid to provide for the family. As an example of how far he had come in his life, Earl told the class that, a few years before, he had been able to buy his mother a house just like the one she used to work in.

Earl related that he had had many tough choices to make at an early age, and many temptations. But he chose to build a legal enterprise and he had created a good life for himself and his family. "Like most young people I speak to these days, many of you are likely at a crossroads in your life," he said. "Let's face it, if and when Julie invites me back, some of you will not be here — based on the decisions you will make today and tomorrow. Some of you will go on to college in a few years and — according to statistics — several of you just might not be alive. Your life is about your choices. So my last questions for you are: What are you going to do? What choices are you going to make now that will determine your future?"

Kids like Deshaun have so much potential and so little support and training on how to succeed after high school. With one in three young people living in poverty, how will they beat the odds and build their competitive edge? Deshaun and others like him are the reason why I left corporate America at age 22 to work for NFTE. I quickly found, after participating in a few classes, that kids like Deshaun began to see that they had the tools to become economically productive. "Don't you see the opportunity we have here?" Deshaun would ask his classmates. "Pay attention. We are lucky to be the first kids in Brockton to get this chance to become entrepreneurs."

* * *

As we all know, stories of people overcoming disadvantaged beginnings to succeed are a hallmark of America. Countless immigrants have come to the United States and fought for the opportunity to accomplish what people like Earl Tate have achieved. My own family's experience has certainly shaped my life and motivated my involvement with NFTE.

After World War II, my grandfather, Nandor Szilard, ran a store selling supplies and household goods in his native Hungary. My grandfather loved being in business for himself. He had escaped from a slave labor camp during the war in the early 1940's and went into hiding. The Nazis murdered many members of our family, including Nandor's in-laws, at Auschwitz. After having escaped the murderous clutches of Hitler's henchmen, Nandor began rebuilding a life for his wife and five-year-old son — my dad.

However, one day, a group of Communist Party officers from the government installed by the Soviet Union paid him a visit. "Is this your store?" Nandor proudly answered, "Yes it is." He was ordered to get his coat and leave. Under the new Communist regime he could no longer own a store. My grandfather had no choice. Everything he had been building was snatched from him in the blink of an eye and there was nothing he could do. How would he provide for his family?

But Nandor was a survivor.

He began making tablecloths and other items that quickly became famous in the Hungarian embroidery industry. My father's room was his manufacturing plant. My dad remembers needing to open the windows in the wintertime because the odor of the chemicals was so strong. It was often necessary for the entire family to work until two in the morning to make ends meet. Nandor rose at 4 a.m. every day to sell his wares at the country market.

Even though my grandfather found a way to run a business in Communist Hungary, he was not allowed to let it grow. He would carry and sell his own wares until he died, at the age of 77. My father, meanwhile, was initially told he could not go to college — despite being a "straight A" student and ranking first in his class. After much persistence on his part, he was finally accepted into law school in Budapest, in 1956. As a young entre-preneur himself, he had sold postage stamps to pay for an English tutor and purchase Shakespeare's *16 Plays*. My father escaped the ill-fated Hungarian Revolution of that year by jumping on a Red Cross bus on its way to the Austrian border. He was 18. He wanted a better life. He wanted freedom.

Hearing rumors that all vehicles would be stopped at the border, and realizing that he might be killed, my father and others left the bus and crossed the wooded frontier late at night. A Hungarian farmer took pity on them, giving them food and letting them spend the night in his barn (and of course risked his own life by doing so).

My father got across the border and somehow made it all the way to Washington, D.C. Jewish Social Services helped him get placed, as a refugee, with a family to whom we will always be indebted — the Levys. He worked at bagging groceries at a Giant supermarket for a year, while he tried to improve his English. My father applied to ten colleges. Although he was turned down by nine, his one acceptance was to a particularly good one — Harvard — on a partial scholarship. He washed pots and pans in the school cafeteria to help pay for his tuition and graduated *magna cum laude* and Phi Beta Kappa in three years, going on to Harvard Law School. After graduation, my father worked for more than 30 years as a lawyer at the International Monetary Fund and The World Bank, and then retired happily to his paradise in Maui, Hawaii, with my wonderful stepmother, Monique.

My family's experiences are an important reason that I so strongly believe in the *I can* (American) dream. It was a sad thing when I found out that so many of the Brockton students' families did not see opportunity in this country. On a NFTE pre-test, I asked my class whether we lived in a Socialist, Communist, or Free Enterprise System. After explaining the differences between the three, 85% thought we lived in a Socialist or Communist economy. When I asked why, they answered: "Because we get everything from the government."

Many of my students' families were on welfare and did not have jobs. They had a feeling of entitlement about receiving government benefits. One young man told me how, in his neighborhood, you could own a car but it couldn't be worth more than $1,000 or else you would lose your welfare benefits— which of course meant you were probably going to own a very substandard car.[1]

Like my dad, many immigrants have risked their lives to come to America for the opportunity to receive an education and try to better themselves financially. In some communities, such as the Korean, friends and family pool money so a relative or friend can open a small grocery store, often working 16 to 18 hours a day to make it a success.

This realization has strengthened my vision and has given me energy to teach the American Dream to young people who need to hear its message. Studies show that 30% of those who start businesses do so because a parent owned a business. But without such a role model for success, kids like those I taught in Brockton will most likely have a tough time envisioning a way

---

1 With the federal government determining the poverty threshold of $19,307 a year for a family of four, our NFTE students need to make over $64 a day (300 days a year) just to "exit" poverty — although I would estimate that $75 to $100 would be closer to the truth. With $19,307, a family of four would not have enough money for life insurance, gifts, school books, shoes, clothes, or many other necessities (See Appendix 3: Budgeting for Poverty).

out of welfare dependency or, worse, a life of crime. So my personal mission became to channel *I can't* into *I can*, through teaching entrepreneurship.

LESSON LEARNED

Many young people have not been exposed to the concept of personal ownership. To move our disadvantaged youth from poverty to prosperity, every high school in America needs to teach financial and entrepreneurial literacy.

CHAPTER 2

The Power Of
Chance Meetings

*Sometimes you meet someone who — like a good
book — opens up a whole world you never knew
existed, and your life is never the same again.*
— Adam Sidel, President, Brainstorm Creative Resources

I watched a well-dressed, confident teenager work the room like a pro — meeting people, shaking hands, making eye contact, and handing out business cards to a prestigious crowd of older, successful entrepreneurs. He was one of several inner-city youth I had noticed at this Inc. 500 Conference (which annually recognizes the 500 fastest-growing companies in America).

I was there working for the conference sponsor, *Inc.* Magazine, the top publication in the country for small but growing companies. It was my first job out of college. And 1991, the year I started with *Inc.*, happened to be the 10th anniversary of the conference. It was held in Des Moines, Iowa and I wasn't really supposed to be there.

"Who are these dynamic teenagers and what are they doing here?" I wondered, as the young man who was selling watches, ties and women's scarves approached me.

"That's a very nice suit," he said. "I've got some beautiful scarves that could really enhance it."

He said the right thing. I had just bought this navy-blue pant suit at Filene's Basement especially for the conference. He handed me his business card, which read: *Terrell Johnson, President, TJ's Accessories, Newark, New Jersey.* I asked Terrell if I could see his scarves, and how much they cost.

"They're $10 each, but I'll sell you two for $16 — conference special," he said with a grin that made me think I might buy four.

We started talking and it turned out that Terrell was all of fifteen. I picked out two scarves and handed him a 20-dollar bill. "Hey, would you like to see my business plan?" he asked, as he handed me my change and receipt. I looked over his plan and noticed he had bought the scarves in New York for $36 a dozen ($3 each!). Now that I knew his "cost of goods sold," which should be classified information for an entrepreneur, I thought less of my big price break — conference special, huh?

But now that I was in his confidence, Terrell told me he typically made $7 on each scarf, and he walked me through sections of his business plan, including his "economics of one unit" page. On his monthly income statement, Terrell showed me that he grossed about $700 each month, but explained he could not keep much of that money as it went towards his monthly costs of doing business and also helping his family out financially.

"I haven't taken out my USAIIR yet!" he said.

"Your USAir?" I asked, curious what he meant.

"Yes, like the airline," he replied. "It stands for my operating costs. You see," he paused to compose himself as if he were standing on a podium at a spelling bee, "U stands for Utilities, S stands for Salaries, A is for Advertising, I stands for Interest and Insurance, and R is my Rent."

I had to smile. Here I was, working for the premiere small business magazine in the country, and this 15-year-old knew more about actual business than I did! I finally had to ask: "What are you doing here at the conference?"

Terrell told me that he had graduated from a program designed to teach inner-city kids how to start their own businesses. (Much later, I realized that his business plan represented Terrell's exit strategy from poverty.) "You need to meet Steve and C.J.," he said, when I asked how I could get involved.

"Steve" was Steve Mariotti, the founder of the program Terrell had mentioned. "C.J." was Chris Meenan, one of the program's teachers and Steve's close associate. Steve was to be the keynote speaker at the luncheon the next day. Little did I suspect at that moment how this encounter with Terrell and hearing Steve speak was going to completely change my life.

After receiving an MBA from the University of Michigan, Steve Mariotti had received a fellowship to study Austrian economics at the Institute for Humane Studies, and then worked at Ford Motor Company as the treasury analyst for South Africa and Latin America. But, feeling frustrated with the limitations of working in a corporate hierarchy, Steve pulled up stakes and moved to New York to open an import-export firm.

Steve spoke very compellingly about how good it had felt to be president of his own company, and how the world and opportunity seemed to open up to him. "It was no longer, 'She went to Stanford so she is smarter than me,' or, 'He is taller so he is better than me,'" Steve said. He realized he could do business with anyone, and that he had something to offer. Starting his own successful business had greatly enhanced his self-esteem.

But, as with many of the lives he had touched — such as Terrell's — Steve's story was also about personal transformation: how an unfortunate event had forever altered his life, and how confronting his personal fears put him on the path to success as a social entrepreneur. In 1981, he went for a run in New York and was beaten up and robbed by a group of teenagers. After the mugging, Steve felt fearful around kids. This really bothered him, especially because both of his parents were teachers. As a businessperson, he didn't understand why those kids had to push him around for a few dollars. "Why didn't they just try to sell me something?" he wondered. In Steve's recovery therapy following the incident, he was encouraged to face his fears:

> *As a way of working through this traumatic event, I gave up my import-export business and began a career as a special education teacher in New York's most difficult neighborhoods. My first year was almost as traumatic as the mugging. I was assigned remedial students, and in each of my classes there was a group of six or seven whose behavior was so disruptive that I had to stop the class every five minutes or so to get them to quiet down.*

*One afternoon was particularly upsetting, to the point
where I had to walk out of the classroom. I thought
about just quitting. But suddenly I walked back in and,
without any introductory comments, launched into a
mock sales pitch for my own watch, "selling" it to the
class. I enumerated the benefits of the watch. I explained
why the students should purchase it from me at the low
price of only six dollars. The class quieted down and
became interested. I didn't know it at the time, but this
incident, born of desperation, pointed me toward my
real vocation — teaching entrepreneurship to low-income youth.*

He later taught a class at Jane Addams Vocational High
School in the South Bronx, with 18 students who had been court-
ordered out of their regular classrooms. He worked with them
off-site, imparting everything he had learned from his MBA
courses at Michigan, but modifying it to make it more accessible,
and more fun.

*Before long, I began offering a special entrepreneur-
ship class and I noticed that even the most disruptive
students settled down and began learning, about business concepts but about reading and basic math, too.
In my last teaching assignment, in the notorious "Fort
Apache" area of the South Bronx, a hundred percent of
my students started small businesses and reported that
they had experienced a major positive change in their
lives. The difference entrepreneurship seemed to be
making in their behavior was incredible.
Eventually I noticed among my students that chronic
social problems — such as absenteeism, dropping*

17

*out of school, pregnancy, drug use, drug dealing, and
violent behavior — had all been significantly reduced.*

The overwhelming success of his Jane Addams project gave
Steve the confidence to launch NFTE — in 1987 (it received
nonprofit status from the IRS the following year). Today (2006),
NFTE has year-round programs both here and abroad that serve
over 22,000 children annually through a curriculum that is often
referred to as a "Mini-MBA" program model.

Steve looked beyond the stereotypes. He learned that 95%
of the inner-city youth he worked with wanted the same things
we all want — to make their families proud, go to college, own a
house, and a car — but very few had a tangible path to get there.
He also learned that, in certain communities, once kids had been
placed in special education programs in high school — where
they receive labels such as "learning disabled" or "emotionally
handicapped"— only one in 20 actually graduated.

To illustrate the gravity of the problem in our public school
system, Steve instructed the 800 people in the audience to "Close
your eyes. I want you to visualize 10 University-of-Michigan-
sized football stadiums filled with young people between the ages
of 15 and 19. Can you visualize this? Over a million kids. That is
the number of teenagers in our country who have dropped out of
school and are unemployed." After a moment, Steve asked us to
open our eyes. "This to me is one of the biggest problems in
America today," he said. "This is a national security issue."

A man sitting next to me at the table put down the conference agenda he had been highlighting a few minutes earlier. A
woman across the table put down her pad and paper and slid her

day planner into her briefcase. Steve had our undivided attention.

"Has anyone in this room ever been laid off or fired?" Steve asked.

A few hands went up amidst a scattering of nervous laughter.

"As an adult, it can be a very painful, nerve-wracking experience, right?" Heads nodded in agreement. "*Now,* I want you to imagine being 16 or 17 without a job or a high school diploma. You have dropped out of school, are unemployed, and have few, if any, skills to make it in a market economy."

"Of these million children who have dropped out of school and are unemployed — a small percentage, perhaps it's 2%, maybe 5% — are in so much psychological pain that they become destructive, and in some cases violent. Some of them have weapons, which makes none of our lives as safe anymore."

Steve pointed out that the only business training most urban public schools had offered in the past was typing, or perhaps some data entry. It was often the typing teachers who ran the "business departments." This seemed tragic, as inner city youth often develop "street smarts" (a willingness to take risk and mental toughness) just to survive. We have found time and time again that "street smarts" can be channeled into "business smarts," with risk taking being a hallmark quality of an entrepreneur. These are the attitudes and abilities that make them ideally suited for breaking out of the cycle of dependency that so often comes with poverty and for getting ahead in the marketplace."

The lights dimmed in the ballroom and the face of Peter Jennings appeared on two movie screens that came down from the ceiling: "This is the story of a teacher who wanted to turn kids away from a world full of drugs, and the kids themselves, who had the guts to reach for a different dream," said Mr. Jennings. These video clips, from ABC's *American Agenda*, went on to profile three NFTE students in 1987, and then follow up with them a year later. One had given up selling drugs to start a legitimate small business. A young woman who had been at a third-grade reading level was selling lingerie at New York City flea markets. The skills she learned to successfully run her business had taught her to add, subtract and keep accurate records. She made $10,000 her first year in business, then went on to work as a bank teller in Los Angeles.

I sat there dumbfounded. I remembered my first job at the age of 11 and what it felt like to be valued and have someone believe in me. Steve's vision and belief in these young people — that they could channel their passions and hobbies into their own small businesses, and build their self-esteem in the process — resonated deeply within me. This mission was possible, I thought. It was simple, it was clear, and it made sense.

At that moment, I knew I would find a way to help Steve's organization grow, even if it was on a small scale. I made a mental commitment to myself then and there to get involved and to say *yes* to this great mission of NFTE's, and to study the path of a social entrepreneur — an individual who builds with two bottom lines in mind: financial viability and fulfilling a social mission.

Terrell, the young man I had bought the scarves from, went up to the podium and shared how he was helping his mother buy groceries with the money from his new business. Another young man talked about how he stopped selling drugs after several of his friends had died. As the last student finished speaking, the audience began applauding. The kids and Steve received not one but *three* standing ovations. I looked around and many people were teary-eyed. We were all collectively blown away!

* * *

Now Steve and I differ on the next part of this story. He will tell you that I went up to him after his speech and said, "I'm going to come work with you — *next week!*" and he will proudly tell people that's when I started. While I do like his version better, mine is a little different.

After graduating from Simmons College, I was hired by *Inc.* as a marketing assistant and fulfillment manager. My responsibilities included managing the fulfillment house hosting some 60 of *Inc.*'s award-winning products that helped people build businesses, and managing the promotions through the telemarketing agency NeoData. Though the job was not a writing position, as I had originally hoped for (I was the editor of my college literary magazine), I considered it a challenge and a way for me to get a foot in the door with a great company. I was proud of earning my first salary (a whopping $19,000), having my own office on Commercial Wharf — which looked out over the water of Boston harbor — and working with a team of bright and pleasant colleagues. I was quite excited about my first foray into the "real world," where I could make my mark.

I was aware of the buzz permeating the building as the day of the Inc. 500 Conference approached: people were planning, phones were ringing, and airline tickets were being booked. I was really excited. This was going to be a gathering of the some of the top entrepreneurs in America! But then I discovered that my department usually did not go to the conference, with the exception of my manager. Rather than just give up, my entrepreneurial side came out. I asked my manager if there was a possibility that I could attend the conference to see and learn more about how the company worked. We negotiated a deal: I would attend the conference in exchange for marketing *Inc.*'s videos, books, and software at the makeshift company store, and taking five or six rolls of photographs of the event.

After we returned from the conference, I asked the head of the department if I could ship the full set of *Inc.* videos and books to the NFTE offices. I sent out six sets (worth more than $6,000) one to each of the NFTE executives I had met at the conference, so they could share them with their teachers and students. Soon I began speaking with these NFTE staff members on the phone almost weekly, to find out other ways we could assist their organization.

My older brother Tony had just returned from a two-year stint in Kenya with the Peace Corps, and a conversation with him inadvertently helped me realize what I wanted to do next. I had written to Tony about the possibility of him teaching youth entrepreneurship when he came home. He had been a young entrepreneur himself after all, selling comic books, baseball cards, and more. He also had powerful leadership qualities. We had a long conversation while walking on the National Mall in Washington, during which I told him NFTE was an amazing organization and right up his alley. After a ten-minute, best-sell monologue on all the reasons he should abandon everything else and teach kids entrepreneurship, I realized it wasn't going to happen. In a last-ditch effort, I said: "Tony, if I wasn't working at *Inc.*, let me tell you, NFTE would be my ideal job!" I didn't realize it a the time how prophetic those words were.

At that time, a man named Mike Caslin was a consultant for NFTE, helping to build a presence throughout New England. Whenever we spoke, he offered me encouragement about my career. One day he called to ask me to be the featured speaker at a summer program, being held in Hyannis, for low-income youth who lived year-round on Cape Cod. (I didn't know there was poverty on the Cape, but there was and still is.) I didn't feel qualified enough to speak as a "business expert," so I asked George Gendron, the editor-in-chief of *Inc.*, to join me. George said yes, but at the last minute had to cancel due to an important meeting. I packed up my car with magazines and videos that morning, ready to drive 90 miles to speak to a group of young people. I felt inadequate for the job, but did not want to let either the kids or Mike down.

There were 50 students in two classes at the local high school, and I spoke 30 minutes or so in each room. The students wanted to know what kind of car I drove, what I did, what my business was. I told them about my job — that I wasn't an actual entrepreneur — but I did share stories with them about my life and all the "business" initiatives I worked on when I was young, from lemonade stands to car washing to door-to-door selling of toys and hair products.

I found teaching fun and a rewarding change from office life. The students were animated and asked interesting and provocative questions. I handed out all my business cards and, as Mike walked me to my car, he talked about his strategic plans to grow NFTE in the area. "We are building a movement, not a monument," he said. He invited me to become more involved as a volunteer, and I told him I would.

The next day I returned to the magazine with five or six stories of the kids I had met and the new businesses they were aspiring to start. A week later I received a package in the mail with three photos and 49 letters. Here are a few quotes:

"Thanks for taking time out of corporate America for me!"

"It's nice to see a young woman in business."

"You know, when you spoke about washing cars, making jewelry and all the things you used to do — I think you are an entrepreneur, you probably just don't realize it."

"I'm going to build my own hair salon one day with a nightclub upstairs and a coffee shop. I want to be the next Madam C.J. Walker ... maybe you could call me sometime ..."

I shared these letters with my department head. Some were so compelling we thought perhaps the magazine could publish them.

As the lowest on the totem pole in the *Inc.* Business Resources Department (IBR), I opened the mail each day. Every week I would get letters from people who wanted to resell the *Inc.* videos and other products we produced. We had a wonderful video on Ross Perot — his business and political views — from a keynote address at a past Inc. 500 Conference. It was at this time that he was declaring his candidacy for president of the United States. I wondered if we could sell the video to the people who would be supporting him.

Some 95% of revenues for our products came through the promotional ads we placed in the magazine. With the blessing of my manager and the vice president, I was finally given the green light to take on some extra projects, such as what we'd do to market the Ross Perot video, and contact people who wrote to us and wanted to resell our products as distributors. This permission led to setting up national and international distributors for *Inc.*, which over the years provided a very strong revenue stream. Most of the people who contacted me and with whom I met were entrepreneurs, and I loved dealing with them — especially the man who wrote to me to say that it was a life or death matter: our videos needed to be sold in Denmark!

My title changed to manager of fulfillment and distribution, yet I was still responsible in the marketing assistant role. Looking back, I might have been a little naive about the impact my changing role would have on my senior colleagues. Here I was, the new assistant, and I was traveling to the Inc. 500 Conference and building these relationships with the American Express Catalogue, Nightingale Conant, and other organizations. One of my co-workers complained that she was confused by my new position; after all, wasn't I her assistant?

The manager of IBR wrote, in her review of my work: "I think Julie would like to bypass an entry-level job and become director of a company. My advice to her is to be happy with where she is." I was really saddened by these comments. I had been working late every night, believing I could do it all. I loved my department, and I really felt that I was being a team player and showing "intra-preneurial" spirit.

A few days later, my manager called NeoData and discovered that the records for the promotions that month were not in their computer system. It was my responsibility to send this information out monthly and make sure it had been received. The next day I was fired.

I felt like I had just been pushed out of an airplane. I hugged my manager, thanked her, and asked if I could stay on for two more weeks to train my replacement, as I didn't want to leave things hanging with the distributors and the relationships I had built. She agreed. I had never really failed at anything before. I was trying to build, trying to show eagerness and ambition (qualities that worked well for me in leadership positions at school) and somehow I totally blew it. I felt worthless. I had just graduated from college and I had already gotten myself fired!

"Julie, why is it that you feel you need to come up with a million-dollar idea every week?" my therapist had asked me a week after I lost my job. At the time, I didn't have an answer for her; I just knew that for some reason that's how I was wired. I was the captain of the softball team during my senior year at Sidwell Friends High School, and every time I went up to bat I knew I would swing my hardest and go for it. Entrepreneurship is more than just about making money; it's about playing the game of life, and to me, now, it is also about personal freedom.

We received a letter from NeoData a few days later apologizing for a computer glitch, that in fact they had received the data in question but it had been lost. The last line was a bit ironic: "We apologize for any inconvenience that this has caused you and your staff." I was lucky to have been able to see the letter, but it was too late to salvage my job.

* * *

One day, early in my time at *Inc.*, I had another chance encounter that led to a relationship that would impact my life for the next 11 years. I was making photocopies when I noticed a man I had not seen before waiting patiently in line behind me. He was wearing khakis and a blue polo shirt, and appeared to be in his mid-fifties.

"Hi, my name is Julie Silard and I'm new in the IBR Department," I said, in a typical display of my outgoing personality; I extended my hand in greeting. "So, um, what department do you work in?"

The man smiled at me with amusement combined with warmth, then shook my hand. "Hi, I'm Bernie Goldhirsh," he said.

Oops. Bernie Goldhirsh was the founder and <u>owner</u> of the magazine. My face must have turned 30 shades of red. I asked him to please go ahead of me, yet he insisted I go first. We chatted for a few minutes and he was very friendly, asking me questions about my background and how my first weeks on the job had been going.

A few days before my departure from the magazine, Bernie Goldhirsh came by my desk. "I heard what happened," he said. "Would you like me to see if I could get you a job in another department?" As it turned out, there weren't any openings, but I was moved and appreciative that he had asked, and surprised when he personally followed up with me several times.

Sometime after the conference, I made a gift for Bernie. I had spelled out *Inc.* with a large, nineteenth-century type face, photographed it and printed it in black and white in the Simmons darkroom. I then sepia-toned the results, to create an old-fashioned brownish color and gave it to Bernie, who then displayed it prominently in his office for many years. Despite what happened at *Inc.*, Bernie later became one of my board members and a key mentor when I started to build the NFTE program in Boston. He donated $19,000 that first year (the equivalent of my annual salary at the magazine!). When his wife passed away — a few years before he did — he asked me if I would spend some time with his daughter. There was a connection there that meant something to him and that I valued very much.

As I walked along Commercial Wharf, leaving *Inc.* for the last time, I had conflicting thoughts about my experience there. To make it on the corporate ladder, I thought I might have to change my ways and become savvier about the hierarchies and idiosyncrasies of operating within a company. But if I wanted to be an entrepreneur, maybe I was on the wrong ladder. Maybe it was time for me to step up and "say yes" to a new calling. Maybe it was time for me to follow my gut instincts and become a social entrepreneur.

* * *

LESSON LEARNED

Sometimes you need to follow your intuition and seize opportunity where it lies. That may mean going places and meeting people you didn't plan on. If you follow up with them, though, magic may occur. Never, ever give up on yourself and, even if you fall, by all means, get back up!

CHAPTER 3

My First Class: Westside Alternative

Two men look out through the same bars:
one sees mud, and one the stars.
— Frederick Langbridge

Mike Caslin, NFTE's consultant in New England at this time (and now our national CEO), was from Mattapoisett, a small town about 60 miles from Boston. I called him during my last week at *Inc.* "I want to come work for you and NFTE between jobs, as a volunteer," I said. "I believe in what you're doing. I could be your assistant or secretary."

"Welcome," Mike warmly responded, and then added: "You can come work with me, but it won't be as my assistant or secretary, it will be as my associate and friend."

My first day with Mike was October 13, 1992. My initial commitment was two days a week, because I had the goal of getting three weekly job interviews as well. The mornings that I made the drive to Mattapoisett, I found myself eagerly anticipating another day of working with Mike and his small team. By the third week, I was working with Mike full time and cancelling my job interviews.

Mike had a small office with wood paneling full of photos of him with Jack Kemp, Ronald Reagan, and other prominent politicians. The four of us shared an open space and would compete to use one of the two working computers. We were trying to build a full-time NFTE program in New England. I set up meetings for Mike and myself for several days a week, and I had responsibility for the follow-up.

Mike taught me how to expand my vision and dream of reaching thousands of young people. He often asked me to map out action plans for how I would meet this challenge and then to run them by him. I was pretty nervous: What if I wasn't smart enough to develop a master strategy?

One day, at Mike's recommendation, I did an hour-long coaching session at a local Burger King with a 17-year-old NFTE program alumnus named José Albert. José revised his business plan for the session and we went through it page by page. He asked me how he could expand his business venture beyond selling electronics and football jerseys to friends in between classes. We discussed setting up a booth at his church or at the New Bedford Mall. Perhaps he could negotiate getting a few feet of space at an existing kiosk at a nominal rent.

"You've got to *want* to succeed," I said to José, and was reminded of the story of Les Brown, a well-known radio personality and motivational speaker. Les grew up in the rough Liberty City section of Miami. When he was a young man, he showed up at a local radio station, looking for a job. The station manager said he couldn't hire Les, since he had no experience. Les pointed out that if no one gave him an opportunity, he would never get any experience. The next day, Les showed up again. "My name is Les Brown and I'm looking for a job here," he told the station manager.

"Didn't I tell you yesterday that there were no jobs?" the manager replied.

"Well, yes," Les answered, "but I thought perhaps someone got fired or quit."

"No," the manager said. "No one got fired or quit." José laughed and said, "I can't believe he went back — *man!*" I continued the story.

Well, the next day, as if he had never been there before, Les showed up at the radio station again, dressed for success, and asked the manager for a job.

"Les, didn't I tell you yesterday *and* the day before that there are no jobs here?"

"Yes, but I thought perhaps someone died or something."

"No. No one quit, no one got fired, and no one *died*. There are no jobs here."

So, the next day Les went to the station manager's office again.

This time the exasperated manager said, "Come in and get me some coffee or something — make yourself useful."

Les went on to become one of the most famous radio personalities and motivational speakers in America. José understood the importance of the story. No one will hand success to you on a silver platter. If you have dreams, *you* have to go after them.

* * *

My mother's father, Mark Massel, whom we affectionately call "Cookie Boge" (his childhood nickname was Bogo, which we shortened to Boge, and added the "Cookie" because he would often bring us cookies when he visited), was an economist, a senior accountant on the staff of the Brookings Institution in Washington, D.C., having previously been a partner with a prominent Chicago law firm. While practicing law in Chicago, he invested in one of his client's businesses, a small family-owned company that was at risk of going bankrupt. He was one of the few non-family members who held an equity position (ownership) in the company, and he eventually became a board and executive committee member. The company, Sanford Inc., sold office supplies that included Sharpie pens (the permanent markers), dry-erase boards, and those great-smelling "Mr. Sketch" markers that included cinnamon (brown), sour apple (green), and cherry (red).

Sanford was sold when I was 16. With the money from his investment, plus other funds he had saved, my grandfather was able to pay for his six grandchildren to go to college and thus give them a better chance when they started out in the world. That money enabled me to take some risks that ended up having a return on investment that has been off the charts!

At the time of the sale of Sanford, my mother was teaching

at the high school I attended, Sidwell Friends — an eternally positive and cheerful single mother of three. We did not have a great deal of money, but we did not want for anything. I bought my clothes at Sears and dinner was often enjoyed at Roy Rogers or Shanghai Delight, and my father helped out a lot. To my brothers and me, life seemed good!

In 1984, when my mother received money from the sale of Sanford, I was involved in my latest venture, shining shoes at the JW Marriott Hotel. I paid rent to run my business but was able to keep all the profits and could have free meals when I was on the job, at the staff dining hall at the hotel. I kept growing my business after my family inherited this money because I wanted to build and create a life like my father had; I did not want to be a spoiled brat and expect everything to be given to me. Now, looking back, I see the great gift of family wealth and how it can position you to take key risks in life. I also see the great gift of having purpose in one's life.

You see, at the time there was no job for me with Mike Caslin and NFTE; I was an unpaid volunteer. But, due to Grandpa Boge's foresight, I was able to spend several months without pay, or the certainty of a job, to help build NFTE from a summer program to a year-round operation in the New England area. I didn't know exactly where I was going professionally at the time, but I knew that something felt right. My friends and family wanted me to "get a real job," but I would shrug off their comments with an "I just have a feeling about this" speech. Within a few months I was made the assistant director — still unsalaried, but Mike always added me as a line item in any grant application he wrote.

I have known Mike for 15 years now, and there has not been one day in which he has treated me any differently than he did from day one — as his *associate* and his *friend*. Mike believed in me and gave me a chance. When he took me under his wing, it started me down a path that would teach me how to "walk the walk" and teach thousands more to do the same: A ripple effect. I will be forever grateful for the opportunity Mike gave me. I understand that I was tremendously fortunate to be in a position to follow my heart and take risks. It might not have happened without my grandfather's entrepreneurial initiative — investing in dry-erase boards and Sharpie pens!

* * *

The first funds we raised for NFTE in New England were through a $20,000 grant from the Island Foundation (whose president, Jenny Russell, ended up teaching me much about how philanthropy works). Once the grant was committed, Mike encouraged me to go through a five-day teacher certification training (called "NFTE University") in New York, taught by Steve Mariotti and C.J. Meenan, held at the offices of American Management Systems.

Steve and C.J. had given each student in the training program $25 to go shopping in New York's Wholesale District, around West 30th Street and Broadway. I bought men's socks and a dozen lipsticks in floral cases for $6. Based on what we bought, Steve had each of us write and defend a business plan. I couldn't believe that "going shopping" was part of my new job. It was a blast! At 50 cents apiece wholesale, I felt I could make an especially good profit on the lipsticks, that I would retail for $2.50 each.

After five wonderful days at NFTE University that left me feeling more confident, Mike encouraged me to negotiate to teach an entrepreneurship course at the toughest school in New Bedford, Massachusetts: Westside Alternative High School (about 70 miles from my home). Within three weeks of my return from New York, I had a syllabus and outline for a three-month, three-day-a-week class at the school.

Migdalia ("Dolly") Morales, a NFTE alumna who had started her own graphic design company, and my good friend to this day, joined me as a junior teacher. The credibility of the program increased dramatically by having Dolly, a young woman who had her own business and lived in the nearby Hillman Street housing projects. An entrepreneurship teacher and a peer from the neighborhood were helping our students learn the ropes, with the addition of a few successful guest speakers who had made millions.

On my first day, one of the teachers poked his head into my classroom to "welcome" me before class started. "These are not the worst kids in the world," he informed me, "these are the worst kids in the universe." I knew that teachers could get burned out, but I decided that each child in my class, and in my heart, was going to start with a 100% clean slate. While I was setting up and laying out the NFTE BizBags — a kit holding textbooks and business tools — that each student got for the course, a young boy with strawberry-blond hair and freckles came barreling through the door.

"Can I stay?" he asked. "They won't let me be here."

His name was Jason, and he was 11 years old. He wasn't enrolled and I did already have 18 in the class, but we had space for 20 so I told him I'd check with the principal's office.

"Give it a shot," they said, "but if you tell Jason something's black, he'll tell you it's white. If you tell him it's blue, he'll tell you it's red. He's a tough one."

"I've got some good news for you, buddy," I said, when I saw Jason in the hallway, "You're *in*! You just need to know that I'm expecting a lot out of you, and I want you to be a leader in the class."

Jason's eyes lit up with a sparkle of pride. He soon became my top student and was usually the first to show up — when we could keep him in class. He was driven, focused, and had an endless hunger to learn. However, he grew impatient and irritable quickly and challenged the older boys at school, so I had to watch him carefully and try to channel his energy toward a project — like his business.

One day Jason came to class early and asked me if I wanted a candy bar. Sure, I thought, why not. It seemed as if he wanted to talk and there were a few minutes before class started. He started to tell me about his life: where he lived, that he had a little sister and an older brother, that his parents worked in retail and he didn't see them a lot, that they worked very hard and he wished they had more time together.

I looked closely at this young man who seemed to be growing up too quickly. I thought that perhaps he was looking for a big sister, an aunt, maybe even a mother figure — or maybe just a friend to care about him. But when the other kids came into the room, he abruptly ended our conversation with a dismissive, "Nice talkin' to you." As time went on, I grew to care for Jason a lot.

After my first week of teaching, the janitor pulled me aside and said that he had been hiding during my classes in the over-sized coat closet connecting my classroom to the hallway. His name was Jim and every day he proudly wore a Boston Red Sox cap and a UMass Dartmouth sweater. He had been hiding as he was afraid there would be a violent outbreak in my class, because it had so many students.

"Those kids are quiet as sheep," he said to me, amazed that they were behaving for the entire 90 minutes.

I hadn't realized that the average class size at the school was only four or five. Walking down the hallways, I would often see classes where each of the kids was reading a different book and the teacher was reading a magazine or newspaper with his feet up on the desk. This wasn't school, I realized, this was a holding pen for kids who got in trouble, a place to keep young people that have been expelled from the mainstream school system.

I thought about the likeable, but fragile, Jason. Sometimes he seemed like a little puppy that just needed someone to scratch his ears. But at other times, if crossed, he could be like an attacking leopard.

* * *

"Let's pretend we're opening a pizza business here in the classroom," I said to the class. "What will we need to get started?"

"Tables," said Ricardo.

"Chairs and a cash register," added Caleb, a 16 year old with tattoos on the back of his neck and who wore an army camou-flage jacket and jeans that hung off his thin teenage hips, revealing cherry-red boxer shorts.

"We'll need an oven, Ms. Julie," said Kyle, "and paper plates, plastic silverware, tomato sauce, cheese."

"Excellent, Kyle."

On the blackboard we wrote a list of 30 to 40 things we would need to start "Kyle's Famous Pizza Parlor," including:

Stove*
Oven*
Menus*
Cash register*
Tomato sauce*
Cheese and toppings (pepperoni, sausage, olives, etc.)*
Paper plates, napkins, and plastic cutlery*
Waiters**
Insurance**
Electricity**
Rent**
Flyers for the grand opening and other promotions ("15% off a large pizza")**
Tables, chairs*
Parmesan cheese, oregano, and hot pepper flakes*
Salad ingredients*
Brownies*
Sodas and cups from BJ's Wholesale Club*

"Now, which of the things we've listed here do we have to buy before our very first customer comes in, before we can make our first sale?" I asked. "In business, these are our start-up costs."

We went back and starred the start-up costs.

"Now, what costs will we have to pay monthly — whether we have one customer in a day or 40?" I asked. "They are fixed every month, like rent. If the rent is $1,100, we'll have to pay it every month no matter how many pizzas we sell." We put two stars next to those and called them our operating costs and overhead.

We discussed the "cost of goods sold." For every pizza we made and sold for $8, we would be paying $2.96 for the pizza box, wax paper, dough, cheese, tomato sauce, pepperoni, napkins, labor time to prepare the pizza, and more.

"Nothing, if I steal it, "said 16-year-old Rashaun. "I can take it home and me and my friends can have a party." The class erupted in laughter.

"Rashaun, don't be a punk," said 11-year-old Daniel, who was sitting next to Jason.

"Shut your little pompous girly mouth," said Rashaun.

Before I could intervene, Daniel had hurled his BizBag right over the table and hit Rashaun in the shoulder. I had set the seats up like a corporate board table so no one would be looking at anyone else's back. Rashaun got up with a snarl and started walking towards Daniel. Jason jumped up, ready to protect his friend.

"*Psych!*" said Rashaun. As I stepped in front of him, he turned and walked back to his seat, receiving high fives from his friends, Benny and Leonard.

I looked at Daniel, who was about five years younger and a good 18 inches shorter than Rashaun, and he seemed relieved. Jason sat down and we continued class, having narrowly avoided the first classroom fight. (I pulled Daniel aside later and I went over the ground rules for the class that we had set on the first day. Throwing BizBags across the room was not OK.)

"Think about starting your own business," I continued with the class, "a company you will own. What types of start-up costs, operating costs, and cost of goods sold will you have? Please write down at least three of each in your workbook on page 49, and then we'll go over your new businesses."[2]

One day Jason's older brother was stabbed in front of his school. Jason was out sick that day at Westside, but I knew he wasn't ill. After he returned, he started getting in more fights. I had to really work with the administration because they realized that he liked the program so much that they were considering removing him from my class as a punishment for bad behavior. On at least three occasions, I had to negotiate to get him back so he could complete the 72 hours and become a graduate (a student has to write and defend a business plan to be an official NFTE graduate).

"Jason, buddy, I need to keep you in this class so you can graduate, "I said, during one of our talks. "Look, if you complete this program, then you will complete junior high, then go to high school. You are so bright — please don't

---

2 The program was not a cure-all. Rashaun's friend Benny, who was in and out of youth detention facilities, was one of two at Westside that did not complete the program. I received a call a few months ago from Dolly about Benny. The *Standard Times* reported that he and three accomplices had been sentenced to life in prison for kicking a man to death during a carjacking.

give up on yourself. I'm not going to give up on you."

Jason gave me the "But they don't understand" speech, then ultimately agreed to do his best not to get kicked out of the class. The next week, Jason decided that his business was going to be selling snacks in the teacher's lounge. Miraculously, the administration agreed.

With funds from the Island Foundation, we took the students on a trip to BJ's Wholesale Club and gave them each $50 to start a company. We then took them to set up bank accounts through a contact Mike Caslin had at Compass Bank — the manager, Clara made sure that each student received the red carpet treatment as a valued customer of the bank.

After doing some market research by interviewing five or six teachers, Jason loaded up on things they needed. His clientele included the principal, whom I grew to like a lot. He was like a former police officer: hard on the surface but underneath I knew he cared a lot about Jason and the other students. It was an amazing breakthrough to watch Jason launch his new company. By selling to the teachers, taking specialty orders, such as trail mix and iced teas, which were not available in the school vending machines, his relationships with the administration began to markedly improve.

The last time I saw Jason, I was driving down the highway and he was pushing a cart from BJ's with his little sister, which held a supply of candy and drinks he would be selling in the teacher's lounge. From time to time I have tried to track down Jason down, but with no luck. The thought of him still makes me smile.

* * *

ENTREPRENEURIAL LESSON LEARNED

To build a business, you need to be prepared to be the Chief Bottle Washer as well as the CEO. It means long hours of hard work, discipline, a willingness to go the extra mile, and taking some risk. Success doesn't come easy, so make sure you are doing what you love to do and then go for it! If you don't want it intensely, you won't get it.

PEOPLE LESSON LEARNED

Sometimes those who seem the most "lost" can be "found" if you believe in them and set the bar high.

CHAPTER 4

Something To Say *Yes* To

*Anyone can hold onto the helm of the ship
when the sea is calm.*
— Publilus Syrus

In late 1994, during my third year of building NFTE in Boston, we received a wonderful opportunity: The owner of the Charles Hotel in the heart of Harvard Square offered, at no charge, to host a breakfast reception to introduce local businesspeople to the organization. The event drew more than a hundred "A-level" attendees that would be of enormous help to me. At this time I was the sole employee of NFTE Boston, working out of my apartment on Longwood Avenue.

One of those key figures was Bill Bygrave, director of the Center for Entrepreneurial Studies at Babson College, in Wellesley. Babson was (and is) the number one school for entrepreneurship in the country. As it turned out, Bill was very touched by one of our students, Kathleen Jeanty, who had spoken about her business of revolutionizing clothing for elderly, arthritic people.

"Because they have arthritis, they can't button buttons," Kathleen had observed during her presentation. "They have to wear those moo-moos, which are so ugly. I want them to look good and feel good, so I am going to use Velcro fasteners, instead."

Here was a high school senior who came to America from Haiti when she was eight, and who never thought she'd be able to go to college. But after Bill, and his colleague Joe Mahoney, heard her story, they encouraged her to apply to Babson, and arranged for a full scholarship. Kathleen graduated, and — after a few false starts — has built a thriving public relations business (Inner Leaf Communications).

Kathleen shared with me recently that entrepreneurship opened her eyes to a whole new world. "When I was in Haiti, I remember watching *Dynasty* and wanting to be like the Carringtons. But I didn't ever know how I'd get there — the car, the home, and the diamonds. NFTE helped me to figure out what I could bring to the table, what I could do. My skill set lies in marketing. I am one of those very lucky people who are doing exactly what she is supposed to be doing and loving every minute of it. Had it not been for NFTE, I might have ended up being miserable working 9 to 5 at some job I didn't like."

I asked her what business meant to her, ten years out of the program. "Now it's not about diamonds and fancy cars; I want to provide for my son [who is seven]. I want to make sure he can go to a good school and not have to worry about it like I worried about it. Had it not been for NFTE, I would have never gone to Babson. I thought just older white guys owned companies. Then I met Jennifer Kushell, and other businesswomen, through NFTE and school. I have had bumps and bruises along the way, but I have two offices now and am hiring two people — things are happening."

Kathleen's success demonstrates the power of networking: you never know who you will meet. Can you imagine how different Kathleen's life would have been had she overslept that day and missed the breakfast?

* * *

After all the presentations and testimonials at the Charles Hotel, something magical happened — the audience *got* it. Several handed me checks on the spot, and others said they would call me to set up a meeting (and they did). So many people in the room wanted to get involved that I felt as if NFTE was being lifted out of my hands and everyone was holding a piece of it. *I was not alone in building this anymore* — and it felt great.

It was only one in the afternoon when I got home after the reception, but I could barely stand. I was emotionally and physically drained — partly from the 16-hour days I had been putting in over the previous few months, and also from the hope I had for the program's success. I could barely get the keys out of my purse to open the front door. Work would have to wait; I needed to take a nap.

When I stepped into my apartment, Zach, my black-and-white tabby, came up and started meowing for food. I fed him and then looked out over my balcony to see Coolidge Corner, a charming shopping area with Tudor-style buildings that always lifted my spirits. Then I noticed that my phone had ten messages. Four were from my junior teaching partner, Dolly Morales. She said to call her — it was urgent! I told myself, O.K., I'll call Dolly, and then I can pass out.

"Julie? It's about Marlin."

Marlin was one of the students from my first class in New Bedford, at Westside Alternative. He was over six feet tall and the class comedian; he was always getting the other kids laughing. He came up to me before the start of each class and gave me a little smile, to let me know that he was there for my protection, if I ever needed it.

"Julie, I have some really bad news," said Dolly. "They just found Marlin's body in a crack house — he was rolled up in a carpet."

My knees gave out and I found myself sitting on the kitchen floor. Staring at the wall in disbelief, I asked Dolly to tell me what she knew. She said she read about this tragedy in an article in the newspaper. We talked for the next 15 minutes, remembering Marlin, laughing together and crying. We were angry that he was dead, and the way the article described him — purple, bloated — that wasn't the Marlin we knew. I didn't know what he was doing there: was he selling drugs, doing drugs, visiting a friend? Dolly and I wondered what we could have done. Did we miss something? Was there something we could have taught him? Had we reached him at all? There was no way to know.

Going from a breakfast of lox and caviar at the Charles Hotel, with over a hundred business leaders who were enthusiastic about youth entrepreneurship, to hearing about a former student found dead in a crack house was too much for one day. I was overloaded and it did not make sense. Then I realized that our work was really just beginning, and it was going to be much harder than I had thought.

* * *

At this time, I was running programs in five neighborhoods in the Boston area. And, while we spent six months searching for rent-free office space, NFTE was taking over my apartment. I literally had BizBags piled from floor to ceiling in my small bathroom, and I would awaken at 4 a.m. to the sound of the fax machine.

Finally, at a memorable board meeting hosted by the Bank of Boston, we got space for our NFTE office after board member Larry Rasky found a spot in the heart of Downtown Crossing, and each board member raised a hand to signal a commitment for one month's rent (today, NFTE New England is located on the Babson College campus). My dear friend Michelle Courton Brown, who at the time was at the Bank of Boston (which funded the high school program at Kathleen Jeanty's school), had me go to a warehouse and pick the furniture for the office, which was a conference room suite above Weight Watchers. Despite my happiness at getting NFTE out of my apartment, during my first day in the office I wanted to cry! There was no one there but me and I knew nothing about putting an office together. I was scared to be doing this alone.

I did get help, though. One of my first student interns was Anton Sanders, whom I had taught, along with his brother Malcolm, at the Roxbury Island School. (I love having interns and temps work at our offices. They add tremendous value to the organization.)

Back when he was 15, Anton had taken me to his church one Sunday. He was also in his high school's ROTC program and I would have trusted him with my ATM card and PIN code. So when he and about 20 other NFTE students came around for an afternoon workshop, I told them the news about Marlin, and how he might have died as a direct result of the choices he had made.

"If you ever find yourself at a crossroads where you could go down the wrong path, I want you to call me," I told them. That same afternoon, Anton took me up on my offer.

"Julie, my older brother sells drugs," he said. "My mother is having a hard time and we might lose our home. I thought I might sell drugs too, just to help my mom out. But after what you told me about that young man who died, I decided I'm not going to."

I looked at Anton, took a deep breath, and hugged him. "I'm very proud of you. Now let's talk about how you can make some money legally, how you can take your business to the next level," I said. Two weeks later we met with our contact at the Downtown Crossing Association and negotiated getting Anton a free outdoor cart so he could sell his wares on the weekends.

I later realized that if Anton — who was among the best and brightest of the children I had taught — would consider selling drugs, than many less resourceful kids in more difficult situations might not even hesitate. There has to be more we can do than tell them to "Just say no." We've got to give these kids tools — something to say *yes* to! Entrepreneurship — starting a revenue-generating legal enterprise — is a "Just say *yes*" concept for youth.

Dolly Morales had developed a powerful lesson on this point. Dolly was a graduate of a summer program run by Mike Caslin in 1991, and he became her mentor (and still is, to this day). She is incredibly devoted to helping other young people, once telling me: "Julie, I want to give to others what the program has given to me — we need to show them a better way!" Dolly wrote up a Life or Death Lesson — a comparative income statement, and together we presented it to our class.

In 1994, Dolly interviewed someone she knew in prison: T.R., a 16-year-old, low-level drug dealer. At the time, Dolly's graphic design business included making and printing business cards for young entrepreneurs in New Bedford. Dolly explained to the students that she currently made $12,000 a year in revenues from her business. Based on her interview with T.R., a young dealer could make $25,000 a year — she cut card stock to manufacture business cards; he cut crack cocaine. She distributed copies of the respective income statements of her business and T.R.'s.

Dolly had to pay Uncle Sam about 25% of her profit. She asked the class if they thought T.R. did. They looked at the income statement and under the Profit before Taxes heading they saw a "0." Of course in the drug industry — an underground economy — one did not pay taxes. Dolly asked the students: "Which of us has a better business model?" Many thought drug dealing was better, since T.R. made $13,000 more than she did — before taxes.

Dolly then asked the class to review the two income statements side by side and assess the opportunity costs. In Dolly's case, she didn't need to carry a gun or beeper, or wear fancy clothes to keep her credibility on the street. She could get insurance to cover losses to her business, but T.R. couldn't. If his inventory was stolen, *too bad*, he'd get no compensation — and he certainly couldn't go to small claims court over a disagreement about a transaction!

Dolly could own a car, whereas T.R. would probably have to lease one because, if he got arrested, the police would likely seize his assets. Dolly also had a lower likelihood of hospital bills, because there was a good chance T.R. would get shot or stabbed in a dispute — which of course could easily be fatal. Dolly could have real friendships with people, whereas T.R. would have to lead a life of subterfuge and lies because at any time someone could "rat him out."

Dolly could carry a business card that read: *Designs by Migdalia: Dolly Morales, President*, and make her family proud. T.R. would not want business cards that proclaimed: *Junior Drug Dealer* and very few people would be proud of him — certainly not his mother or his teachers. Dolly's starting point of $12,000 could grow into a major and profitable business. T.R. could perhaps grow his business too, but he might have to take a few years off for jail time, and the odds were against his surviving very long at all. "Which business is a better model?" we asked the class again.

The cost/benefit analysis spoke for itself.

People have often asked me, "What do you think your biggest competition is?" The answer I usually give is: the illegal drug industry.

* * *

50

After applying three times, in 2000 I was finally accepted into Leadership Washington (the youngest person admitted that year), an organization that connects and challenges leaders in the DC area for the purpose of improving the region's quality of life. We met ten times over the following year to address issues that included education, media, public safety, economic development, arts, and diversity. One day a group of us went to visit Lorton prison. It was filled with men (and an increasing number of women) in their twenties, the vast majority of whom were incarcerated on charges related to drugs.

My eyes were more opened than ever! Kids were filling our prisons. Were many of them entrepreneurs selling the wrong *product*? I wondered if — in survival mode — they just got caught up in the streets at too early an age. So many of our young people in tough neighborhoods are learning street economics — like the eight year old who is offered $50 by some older kid to watch out for the police. I didn't see many lemonade stands on Good Hope Road, in Southeast Washington. I wondered how many at-risk kids there were who could be reached, like Anton — and how many times we would try and fail, as with Marlin.

The illegal drug industry *is* our competition for poor children, although drugs span socioeconomic levels and geographic location (consider the epidemic of meth labs in rural America). The key weapon in the war on drugs should be reaching young people early with *legal* enterprise training to prepare them to make it as productive members of our market economy. We have to train them to examine the cost/benefit analysis of their choices.

* * *

LESSON LEARNED

Many people have asked me if entrepreneurship can actually be taught or whether entrepreneurs are just born. I think entrepreneurship is a fundamental life skill that can and must be taught to everyone. Young people need to learn early on that, whether they decide to work for themselves or someone else, they will have a place in America's market economy through legal enterprise.

CHAPTER 5

Landing Microsoft:
The Rashidi Sheppard Story

Indifference never wrote great works, nor thought out striking inventions, nor reared the solemn architecture that awes the soul, nor breathed sublime music, nor painted glorious pictures, nor undertook heroic philanthropies. All these grandeurs are born of enthusiasm, and are done heartily.
— Anonymous

The Westside Alternative School program in New Bedford was a huge success: 93% of the students wrote business plans and de-fended them to a panel of judges, and 17 of 19 graduated at a beautiful ceremony that included a very proud principal and the superintendent of the New Bedford School District. As a result of our accomplishments, the Island Foundation — which had funded the program there — asked if we would meet with the Roxbury Island School officials and see if we could work together.

The Roxbury Island School (a subsidiary of Thompson Island Outward Bound) was located in Boston. After eight months of putting more than 40,000 miles on my car driving to New

Bedford and Brockton, the idea of a program in Boston itself sounded great! A wonderful man named Desiré Mondon was the program director at Roxbury Island. He was also an entrepreneur who had set up a manufacturing facility behind a storefront in Copley Plaza (an area designated for start-up minority companies) and sold beautiful African-inspired couture and furniture. We sent a grant application to the Island Foundation, which then awarded $20,000 to operate our first after-school program in Boston. When Jenny Russell called me from the Foundation, she said the criterion for funding that year (1993) was "passion," and that we would be receiving the funds to launch this second class.

Things got off to a bit of a rocky start because, unbeknownst to me, Desiré was leaving the school, but wanted to come back to teach the program with me three days a week. We set it up so that on one day a week the class would meet at Copley Square, in the elegant boardroom connected to his store. The Roxbury Island School had assumed we would pay Desiré out of the $20,000 grant, but we had only budgeted about $2,500 for one teacher and thought Desiré was still on their payroll. So we worked out a small stipend for Desiré and he became my first teaching partner in Boston. We worked together for years, including at our first Summer BizCamp, held at Babson College. Along the way, we became fast friends, and have remained so.

A short time into the course, I noticed that a 13-year-old student, Rashidi, who was from Trinidad, was bringing items into the class to sell — one week it was Pokemon cards, the next, it was snack items. He was eager to be in business, even at this tender age! Since there were no stores nearby, we created a break time so Rashidi could sell at his desk, out in the open — he had been sneaking sales to the other students under his desk when he thought I wasn't noticing. He was always wheeling and dealing, so I started to call him "Mr. NFTE" (our acronym is pronounced Nifty). Rashidi was embodying the entrepreneurship drive — and his enthusiasm was infectious. With his friendly smile, he was always ready for the next sale.

One day we had a selling event at Roxbury Island School and the kids handed out flyers to their neighbors. "Step right up!" called out Rashidi at the front door of the school to anyone who passed by. "Come meet some great young entrepreneurs! We are here to meet you! We are open for business!"

A few weeks after the program ended, Rashidi and his friend Anton, the student who had confided in me that he had been tempted to sell drugs, joined me at Inc. World, a conference and trade show hosted by the magazine. Bernie Goldhirsh had given NFTE a free booth to promote the program.

Anton and Rashidi wandered around collecting promotional items — pens, flashlights, and so forth — from the many booths — as well as business cards. They were in seventh heaven, participating in this grown-up professional event. How we connected to Microsoft, which eventually became a multimillion-dollar donor to NFTE, started that very day with Rashidi and Anton.

Our six-foot-wide booth was about 40 feet away from Microsoft's much larger and grander installation. "Hey Rashidi," I said, pulling him aside, "maybe you could go over and meet someone at the Microsoft booth. Perhaps they could help NFTE with some computer software."

Always up for an entrepreneurial challenge, Rashidi grabbed Anton and off they went, practically running down the aisle between booths. I stayed behind so as not to leave ours empty. I saw the boys approach a nice-looking man at the Microsoft display. I couldn't hear what was being said but I saw Rashidi's hands flailing around as he spoke — he was always demonstrative. Then Rashidi and Anton both reached into their wallets and presented their business cards.

Five minutes later, Tom Hartocollis, a high-level marketing executive for Microsoft New England, came walking back with the boys. "Are you teaching these young people how to start their own businesses?" he asked.

Tom and I proceeded to have a great conversation about the organization and its mission, and we exchanged cards. He called me a few weeks later and said that NFTE's mission fascinated him and that he would like to have a meeting with me at his office. As a result of this meeting, Tom agreed to serve on the board of advisors for NFTE Boston and quickly became one of my most active board members. He and his team contacted Tom Stemberg, of Staples, and they set up a computer lab for our students at our newly opened Boston headquarters.

I introduced Tom to Steve Mariotti and Mike Caslin over breakfast at a restaurant at Downtown Crossing. Steve was extremely impressed with Tom, and delighted that he had joined our local board.

A few months later, Tom got a major promotion and moved to Seattle. "I can help you all the more," he said before he left. I felt deprived of one of my star board members. However, I later went out to Seattle to visit Tom and, true to his word, he had secured funding to do a BizCamp in the area. My role was to lay the groundwork and recruit the kids. The national office in New York ran the camp and did an effective job of informing the local media. Around this time, Tom introduced Mike and Steve to Jeff Raikes, who had built the Office software platform, as well as other key Microsoft team members.

The following year, in 1996, NFTE held ten Summer BizCamps, and I found myself in DC, responsible for those held at the universities of Howard and Georgetown (we had two board members who graciously offered their respective schools, so I spent a week at each). All ten were sponsored by Microsoft, and Tom brought Microsoft's current president, Steve Ballmer, to meet with some of our DC BizCamp students. Tom went on to become chair of NFTE's national board of directors, while other Microsoft executives — Bob Jones, Michael Robinson, Allison Watson, Kim Tubbs Herron, Aaron Bernstein, and Keith Solomon (to name just a few) — have been of great help to NFTE in New York, Washington, D.C., and other areas.

While he was networking and gathering promotional items at the trade show, little did Rashidi — Mr. NFTE — realize that he would find one of the organization's largest donors and greatest friends! This event left me more convinced then ever that networking is the key to opening the door for success. Malcolm Gladwell's book, *The Tipping Point* (which I recommend highly), argues that there are people out there who love other people and are natural networkers — they are *connectors*. Find these people and work with them: they can open up worlds that you never knew existed.

A president of a local bank recently suggested that I look at every dollar NFTE has raised locally and figure out who made the introduction. If an individual made key introductions that led to substantial results, I should put them on my personal and internal VIP list, as part of a "circle of influence." Sure enough, in looking through our 385 donors, what they had in common was that nearly all had been introduced to us by the same twelve people. These folks are not silver or gold; they are *platinum* to me — even if they aren't in a strong position to give financially themselves.

***

LESSON LEARNED

Network, network, network! Get out there and meet people. People do business with other people. You never know who you will meet and how he or she could help you, or vice versa. But you will need to learn when to ask for something and when to give something when asked — building relationships is a delicate balance.

CHAPTER 6

Going Home

If we are facing in the right direction, all we
have to do is keep on walking.
—Buddhist Proverb

As I boarded the plane from Boston to Washington, D.C. on that blustery March day, I felt like the tragic heroine in a grainy black-and-white film heading for what the entire audience knew was going to be a bad ending. A few days earlier, I had received a phone call from the NFTE national office in New York that had tasted like aspirin on a dry tongue.

NFTE was turning over its Boston operation to Sean Thomas, a young man they had originally recruited for another city. After that deal fell through, they offered him Boston and he accepted. The organization expressed hope that I would either move to New York to take on a fundraising position at national headquarters, or go to Pittsburgh to be the executive director there. Everything that I knew was about to change — what I had built for NFTE in Boston, my gorgeous new condo — I felt as if a part of me had died.

So I made a decision. After nine years, it was time to come home. My career at NFTE was most likely over and I wanted to reconnect with my roots. I called Mike Caslin while I was waiting for the plane. "Mike, I'm not going to take the position in New York or Pittsburgh. All I know is that I'm moving back to Washington and if I end up leaving the company, I want to thank you for everything you've done for me."

I glimpsed at the city that raised me on our final approach and thought of the beautiful landscape and mild weather. I couldn't stop smiling as I got off the plane, and childhood memories kept coming to mind as the cab drove me home along the Potomac: playing hide-and-seek with my father at Montrose Park in Georgetown; sneaking out of high school for secret talks and cappuccino with my mother; Gigi, the black French sheepdog who slept at my feet; and the memories that I would have to come to terms with, broken families and several father figures who left with my stepbrothers as if they had barely existed.

That Saturday, my real father and I took a long walk around Lake Barcroft, near his home in Falls Church, Virginia, and talked about my predicament and plans. I felt like a pawn on a chessboard and resented being moved around and possibly knocked off. I realized that something in me had changed over the past four years. I liked to build things, even while not knowing if — or how big — they would grow. Mike Caslin had told me that I was an "owner" at NFTE and that as long as I kept everyone in the loop, this would be mine to build. I witnessed how passion, perspiration, heart, dreams, and good people could make things happen — in fact, this way of life was beginning to define me. I couldn't go back to the corporate world. I felt that I had truly become a Social Entrepreneur.

"Dad, I don't know what I'm going to do with my life," I said. "All I know is that I'm moving back to DC. I'll sell my apartment in Boston next month. I'd like to stay with NFTE, but I'm not going to Pittsburgh or New York. Whatever happens, happens."

My Dad said he had a plan for me. "Harvard Business School!" he declared, as we walked by the Canadian geese nesting by the side of lake, as if he had hit upon the answer of all answers. This "solution" exasperated me — but Harvard had been a big part of my father's American Dream, after he escaped from Hungary. I knew he only suggested it because he wanted the absolute best for me.

"But Dad, I would go to business school to learn to do just what I'm doing now," I pointed out. "In the process of getting my MBA, I'd lose the opportunity to get the experience I've been getting."

I had already envisioned a new life for myself in DC, and mentally I had already left Boston, said goodbye to my two best college friends, my board of advisors, my favorite students, and everything else there. I realized that DC was where my entrepreneurial spirit had been born. When I was little, my brothers and I had a lot of energy and we would go door-to-door selling things, washing cars, doing odd jobs to make a little pocket money. I started working when I was 12, through a program offered by Field School (which I attended for a few years) to give students real-life work experience while still in school.

I had worked at a store called Once in a Lifetime, in Georgetown; my mother had met the owner, Karen Cartwright, at an Episcopalian church on Wisconsin Avenue that she often attended with my stepfather. Karen decided to give me a chance and take me under her wing. What was supposed to have been a month-long internship turned into a three-year experience. While she couldn't pay me directly, due to child labor laws, she gave me store credit at a rate of $5 an hour, which is how I bought wonderful gifts for my family on birthdays and holidays.

During my third year working for Karen, she was diagnosed with cancer. She was so sick that on some days I would run the store by myself for eight or ten hours (she would have friends from nearby stores come in and check on me). I felt terrible about Karen and I wanted to really be there for her. I loved running the store: operating the cash register, making promotional signs, unwrapping beautiful new inventory, setting up displays. It amazes me to this day how much responsibility Karen gave me and that she had confidence in me, even though I was so young.

But most of all I loved the feeling of responsibility and having a place to go where I was valued and could be creative. The store was a sanctuary for me at a time when my family life began falling apart. My mother was in a verbally abusive marriage and it was very hard on all of us, especially my older brother Tony, who took the brunt of my stepfather's wrath. Karen introduced me to a different world — an escape from home — that filled me with serenity. She played music by the Japanese New Age musician Kitaro, and taught me about carrot juice and other habits of healthy living that she was utilizing to fight the cancer. She not only survived, Karen thrived, and moved on to feed hundreds of homeless people with meals prepared at her home every day.

I made the decision to get off the corporate ladder and become a social entrepreneur while living in Boston, but the idea of returning to the place where I had grown up and that had nurtured my entrepreneurial spirit seemed more right the longer I was back. I knew I was there to stay. I was happy, and clear about the decision.

* * *

Driving that Monday to a birthday lunch at the Four Seasons with my mother and her best friend, Ina, my cell phone rang. It was Lenny, executive director of NFTE National, and Mike. "Julie, we've been thinking about you and we're sure you've been thinking a lot about us," Lenny said. "We want to have a talk with you." I agreed to call them back from the hotel.

I left Mom and Ina chatting away happily as bitter-sugar squares bubbled up from the bottom of their champagne cocktails. "What should I do?" I wondered. Should I ask if they'll let me work for NFTE from DC, or should I just say goodbye to the company and all that it had meant to me? At the payphone I touched the cool dark granite and took hold of the pen hanging by a chain to note talking points, in case I needed them. To clear my head I took ten deep breaths, closed my eyes, and envisioned the waves at Bethany Beach I loved to play in as a child. Then I made *the call*.

Lenny started the conversation. "Julie, we have been thinking and talking about you, and Mike and I have a question: how would you like to run the regional office in DC?"

"*What?!* Are you kidding?" Was I dreaming? Kevin Greaney was running DC at the time. He was one of my first friends at NFTE — we had met at the Inc. 500 Conference. What I didn't know was that they had called Kevin and offered him the New York regional office to free up DC for me. Kevin owned an Irish pub with some friends in New York, so he was thrilled to be going back there. The dreary black-and-white film I had imagined myself in had unexpectedly changed into a brilliant Technicolor movie. "Yes!" I shouted in the lobby when I had put down the receiver. "I can't believe it, but *yes!*"

The Washington organization was mine to build and I didn't have to leave NFTE. This would be a step up for me both personally and professionally. I let the fact that I was truly valued sink in. I knew that Mike Caslin had to be responsible for this, with Steve's approval. "Mom, do I have news for you!" I said when I returned to the table.

Lenny and Mike explained that DC was the "Taj Mahal" of NFTE's operations. With a benefactor who was donating half a million dollars annually, with office space in Georgetown, funds to hire an assistant, teachers trained, eight program sites serving over 260 youths a year, a great public relations firm (Fleishman Hilliard) on retainer, and a board already in place — I would be in an excellent position to take the Washington operations to the next level.

As it turned out, Sean Thomas lasted only a few months in Boston but luckily NFTE has found outstanding personnel for New England and the program there has thrived.

I realize now that I was burning out in Boston. I didn't know how to get to the next level and was working myself to the bone. But I wouldn't have left on my own — just as I wouldn't have left *Inc.* earlier — because of the loyalty I felt towards what I was building. I can now see that these two seemingly unfortunate events — losing my job at *Inc.* and being displaced from NFTE Boston — became sources of extremely good fortune in my life.

***

LESSON LEARNED

When you are part of a team in a growing organization, the whole team has to do its best to move the organization's mission forward with strategic decisions, while juggling many variables and factoring in many people. In my case, I was fortunate that the team was able to keep me on board and that I was able to let go of my ego for the greater good.

CHAPTER 7

It Takes Many Streams
To Fill The Potomac

If you want to lift yourself up, lift up someone else.
— Booker T. Washington

"Yo, yo, yo, yo, man," said the voice on the other end of the phone in a strong Jamaican accent. "NFTE? Yeah, I'll meet. When can we meet?"

That voice was well known to DC reggae aficionados as "Rude Kid," but it also belonged to a young entrepreneur named Denton Malcolm, who was a NFTE Greater Washington alumnus. I had been trying to track Denton down. I had called his home, only to find out that he was no longer living there. Finally, he had called me from his part-time job at McDonald's and agreed to meet with me the following week.

Denton made quite a first impression. He showed up for our appointment at my new office in July 1995, wearing sunglasses and a leather jacket, looking as if he were ready to step into an MTV video. "Nice to meet you," he said, flashing an absolutely winning smile. "You might have seen me on CNN or in the *Washington Post*," he said, giving his recent media resume. I had seen him on the CNN piece and asked him to tell me about his life.

Denton had graduated from Roosevelt Senior High School, in Northwest DC. It was one of the middle-performing public high schools in the city, and nearly half its student body were eligible for free lunches. Denton had been active in school to say the least: he was president of the senior class and captain of the soccer team, among many other credits. He had flourished in the NFTE program under teacher Marilyn Hollis.

Denton also told me that he was currently homeless.

Over the next hour and a half Denton explained his world to me. After his graduation, his father wanted him to go on to college. He had not been accepted at Howard University, the prestigious, historically African-American school in Washington, but was offered a scholarship to Johnson and Wales, the culinary university in Rhode Island. But Denton didn't want to leave DC and his burgeoning career as a reggae artist. Under his stage name, "Rude Kid," Denton performed late into the night, working part-time at McDonald's during the day, and ignoring his father's threats that he would throw him out of the house if he did not either enroll in school or leave on his own.

"One night I came home at 4 a.m. after performing with Bounty Killer and Capleton at the Zulu Cave," said Denton, referring to a popular venue on "U" Street. "I saw all of my clothes and everything was on the front porch. I didn't think he would do it, but he did." Over the next three months, Denton slept on people's porches — sometimes those of relatives who would not allow him to come in the house out of respect for his father's wishes — in shelters, cars, or anyplace else he could find a place to rest.

Denton and I came up with a plan. With his McDonald's paycheck and a personal loan from me of $250, Denton began buying fashion items he could sell through his own business, RK Productions, after his "Rude Kid" stage name. He started out with perfumes, oils, scarves and watches from DC wholesalers, then went to New York to buy fancy high-end brands, such as Gucci, at wholesale prices. He soon realized that some of the labels were knock-offs, so he changed his line to ensure high quality and affordable prices. His reggae fan base and other local performers became his most loyal customers. In a very short time, RK Productions provided Denton with enough income to rent an apartment.

A magical moment in my relationship with Denton came a few years later, when I was running late for a meeting with the Freddie Mac Foundation. I had just come back to the office after an earlier meeting and was about to jump into a cab, when I realized that I had only $5 in my wallet. I asked everyone in the office, but no one had any cash to lend me. When I ran into the office, Denton had been sitting in the board room making phone calls, holding a three-inch stack of business cards. "I'll lend you some money," he said, having overheard my plight. "Here," he added, pulling a 20-dollar bill off a large roll with a smile. "Now go to your meeting and don't be late!"

Over the years, Denton started many companies, including an event-planning firm, a video business, a window installation company, and a clothing business. Under "Rude Kid" he has been awarded local reggae artist of the year four times, and often speaks at high schools and on the radio about his personal path to success. One of his ventures was financing NFTE alumna Lelani Mitchell, who launched a wonderful company, Celebrity Catering.

Denton has also had a few close calls with fate. Once, after returning from New York with a bag of items earmarked for prospective buyers he was meeting later, Denton was held up at gunpoint right outside his home and lost everything he had bought. In another hold-up attempt, when he had $5,000 in cash to go back to New York, he was shot straight through his thumb as he pushed the gun away from his stomach. The assailants ran off without the money and Denton was rushed to the hospital.

The things that have always impressed me about Denton are his positive outlook on life, his survival skills, and his entrepreneurial drive. He is also very open to constructive feedback. As I've watched Denton grow over the years, I've noticed that he has become much more focused. He came to our house a few months ago for dinner and played with my three-year-old daughter while we talked about his business and later sang karaoke. In the world of business we talk a lot about Return on Investment. The $250 I invested in Denton's dream has given one of the best returns I have ever received!

In fact, Denton's story brings up an important part of NFTE's work that heretofore had been missing — measuring success. Denton was a NFTE alumnus who was struggling to find his way after graduating from our program. Without follow-up, coaching and a personal loan, he might not have landed on his feet.

* * *

The David H. Koch Charitable foundation launched NFTE in Washington, D.C. in 1994, to get the program in the eye of policymakers. A few years later, they hired a New York-based philanthropic research company to study what was becoming of our graduates after leaving the program. They found that 12% of the DC alumni were in business five years after graduating, compared to 8% in Wichita, and 10% in New York — the other two cities that were included in the study. Given minority business formation rates in America, these numbers were twelve times the national average for adults. Five years after graduating, 87% of the DC youths viewed themselves as entrepreneurs, 70% wanted to reconnect with a NFTE executive to discuss actual or potential businesses, and more than 90% would "recommend the program to a friend."

My eyes started tearing as I read the study results. It was inspiring to learn that the program was successful in giving hope to the kids in DC, and that they were more optimistic about their future because of NFTE. A later investigation, by the Harvard School of Education, found that "in the beginning of the course, NFTE students expressed less interest in college and fewer hopes and worries related to college, than the comparison group. After the course, NFTE students' interest in college had increased 32%, while the comparison group's interest had decreased 17%."

One of the needs identified by the Koch study was how to support students like Denton once they became alumni. The research indicated that most had changed their residences, and often more than once, just a few years after graduation and, as a result, were difficult to track down. This presented a real issue about staying in touch with graduates that NFTE still faces today. In 2006, NFTE plans to issue an "alumni card" to everyone who completes the full program, through which it will be possible to receive personal e-mail from the organization so contact can be maintained as well as access to a national alumni resource network.

I had sold my apartment in Brookline, a suburb of Boston, in July 1995 and found a very nice rental unit on "M" Street, in DC's Foggy Bottom neighborhood, from which I could walk to the NFTE Washington headquarters in Georgetown. The office was offered to us gratis by Temps & Company. Steve Ettridge, president of Temps, had heard Steve Mariotti speak for the first time the same day I did, at the 1991 Inc. 500 Conference, and made a commitment to help NFTE in Washington if we ever started a program there.

After running NFTE Boston from my apartment, and personally teaching most of the programs, Washington was definitely a change for the better! In 1994, NFTE Washington DC had trained ten local teachers from a geographically wide area of junior and senior high schools: Cardozo, Anacostia, Bell, Hine, MM Washington, Coolidge, Roosevelt, Woodson, Options Charter School, and the Armstrong Adult Education Center. Over the course of a few weeks I was whisked into meetings at our donor's corporate office, media training, with all the coffee I could ever drink from Temps & Company (they even supplied pro-bono administrative staff from time to time). Most of all, I listened, listened, and listened some more. I met one-on-one with the top board members, and set up a monthly dinner meeting with all of the teachers in the DC program. However, because our major donor, David Koch, was living in New York at the time, I had very limited access to him. His team in the Washington office, however, was accessible and helped me expand the organization on many levels.

Mr. Koch was tall (about six-foot-four) and very direct. He would often come to our awards ceremonies and spend a great deal of time connecting with the young entrepreneurs. The few times I met him, I'd be on pins and needles and would talk too fast just trying to catch him up on our growth and progress. His sister-in-law, Elizabeth, was more accessible. Elizabeth, and David's brother Charles, were very instrumental in NFTE's start up in Washington, as well as in Wichita and Minneapolis. Elizabeth became chairperson of our National board and of the Young Entrepreneurs of Kansas. Sometimes she would share with me what was going on in Wichita. She was so passionate, like a full-time team member, and always seemed willing to go the extra mile for the kids.

I would say with utmost respect that the Koch family probably did more for youth entrepreneurship education in the early 1990's than any other philanthropic operation in America, and helped set a trend that was followed by the Shelby Cullom Davis Foundation, Goldman Sachs, the Kauffman Foundation, the Samberg Family Foundation, Atlantic Philanthropies, and the Harry & Jeanette Weinberg Foundation.[3] I believe NFTE was the only high school or K-12 educational program in the David H. Koch Foundation portfolio at the time, and we have been fortunate to have the support of so many other foundations that share the NFTE vision.

---

3 The latter is making major breakthroughs with the new NFTE office in Baltimore that we built as a satellite of the Washington Region and then turned over to the very able hands of Baltimore Board Chair Larry Rivitz and Executive Director Tricia Granata.

At the end of our two-year funding cycle from David Koch, and about six months after I returned to Washington, we received word that we would need to pursue other revenue sources, that our "seed capital" funding would be coming to an end. We would have to show that there was a market demand for our work in Washington and fly on our own.

We did receive some additional funds from the foundation that were to be targeted to alumni programming, but we would need to attract additional resources immediately. I was worried that we would have to drop the in-school programs. I pondered: How was I going to turn this around? To make things more difficult, my assistant, Kayla, resigned and got another job.

Mike Caslin once said to me that it took more than one stream to fill the Potomac River. A social entrepreneur has to build something of value without regard for existing resources. I still had faith. I was more determined than ever that the DC program would grow. I realized that I had nothing when I started in Boston, so what was the big deal if I had nothing now? This was exactly the kind of challenge I had trained for!

First, I called Anne Allen at the Cafritz Foundation. She had once mentioned something to me about not funding national organizations, and I wondered if she perceived NFTE Washington in that way. Anne offered to meet with me, and soon realized that the advisors on our board were local and that our fundraising was for the support of local programs. The Cafritz Foundation asked for a $25,000 proposal to sustain our DC school sites. A few months later *we received the grant!* We were able to cut some minor corners and save every single one of our program sites, with the exception of one school, which had closed its doors. We didn't drop one class, just modified what we could offer.

A few months later, the Freddie Mac Foundation decided to fund our junior high school programs. Then a local entrepreneur, Ron Haft, announced a $60,000 grant from the Dart Foundation to fund two years of the office space we had found at 733 15th Street, NW, centrally located near the White House (so the kids could get to us by Metro, Washington's subway). At $14 a square foot, it was the best deal in town, and we loved it. Five offices, a computer lab (thanks to donations from four different companies), and a conference room, plus furniture donated by board member Vickie Tassan (then at NationsBank).

To be honest, it felt as if we had gone from filet mignon served on a silver platter to hamburgers with French fries. It was tough and I know that sometimes I was perceived as "the bad guy" — an ambitious, 20-something woman managing teachers twice my age — but ultimately NFTE Washington DC regained its footing and did not lose a program, unless a teacher moved on. However, our teachers remained incredibly loyal, and several even offered to help with the fundraising. Most of our "original ten" are still with us today and, several have since become NFTE legends, such as Mena Lofland (see Chapter 10). We worked with 250 young people in our first year, and then over the next ten years grew to serve some 2,100 annually in the region, including our expansion into Baltimore.

* * *

LESSON LEARNED

Lesson Learned: Winners never quit and quitters never win. To quote Henry Ford, "Failure is the chance to begin again more intelligently" and "Failure is neither fatal nor final." In building a business, you have to plan for setbacks. Have a mentor or a coach — or engage in another activity, like an art class or a weekend at the beach — to help decrease your stress. You are running a marathon, not a hundred-yard dash, so take care of yourself — you do not need to burn out. Watch Rocky *and get the fight — "the eye of the tiger" focus — back in you!*

CHAPTER 8

Thursday, Friday, And Two Cancelled Dates

Our basic common link is that we all inhabit this planet. We all breathe the same air. We all cherish our children's future. And we are all mortal.
— John F. Kennedy

"Why can't Marcus come tomorrow? He's our first-place winner and everyone will want to meet him. *What*? He's been *shot*? Oh my God, is he all right?"

I couldn't believe what I was hearing. Marcus was one of two of Marilyn Hollis's students from Roosevelt High School that had taken first and second place at the NFTE Citywide Business Plan Competition the previous week (hosted by the Advisory Board Company). Marcus's business — custom-designed, hand-painted hats and wearable-art jeans — had greatly impressed the panel of judges. We had scheduled an awards luncheon that was to honor Marcus and the other winners, but instead I would be postponing the ceremony and visiting him in the hospital. Marcus was a drive-by victim, shot while walking back from school after working on sets for a school play. "Being shot wasn't part of the business plan," read *The Washington Post* headline a few days later.

When I saw Marcus at the Washington Hospital Center that Thursday morning in June of 1997, he was somber but surrounded by friends. He had taken eight shots in his legs and hips, but he was going to survive. I had brought a letter with me, announcing that he had been awarded $1,000 to invest in his business. Marcus smiled, but I was dismayed when I saw the apathetic attitudes of his friends in the room, all of whom were in their late teens or early twenties. They did not seem shocked to find Marcus in this state, as many of their other friends had also been shot, and sometimes killed. Perhaps reading my mind, Marcus remarked that none of his friends had jobs. He asked me if I could talk with them about starting their own businesses.

"They won't hire me," said one of the friends, "they won't give us jobs."

Who are "they"? I wondered, yet ultimately understood that they were referring to corporate America.

We talked for the next 45 minutes about what skills each of them had that could be used for starting a business. One liked to videotape parties, another wanted to be a rap artist, and another loved to cook.

"What about starting your own businesses this summer?" I suggested. "Marcus has a business plan template that's *kick butt*! Let's talk."

As I left the hospital I felt older than when I arrived. I realized that these young people were at a crossroads, and that they needed the help of an organization like NFTE if they were going to make it. They needed a mentor. They needed something in their lives to say *yes* to.

In the car driving back to the office, I checked my messages and realized that I was going to have to reschedule the date I had for lunch this Friday. I received a call that there would be a funeral for someone who was very special to me. This was my second rescheduling of this date, as I had cancelled it once before, the day I heard the news about Marcus. This was not a good time for potential romance.

* * *

"Come on you guys, it's all about the 'F' word," I remember Walter Benson, my 48-year-old-board member, saying, standing in front the class dressed as if he had walked out of an LL Bean catalogue — beige pants, navy jacket and a blue-and-crème-striped sailor sweater. After hearing just ten minutes of my lesson plan on time management, Walter had walked to the front of the classroom and grabbed a piece of chalk.

"You know, the 'F' word," he repeated loudly, to the class of about 20 teenagers I was teaching at a summer BizCamp at Howard University. "Do I need to write it on the board?"

This was a tense moment. I wondered if Walter had missed taking some of his medication.

Walter wrote an "F" on the board, left a space, and then wrote a "C."

The eyes of 16-year-old Daryn Dodson, sitting in the front

row, opened wide with amazement. My hands started to move toward Walter's arm, to pull him out of the classroom.

"Now there is a 'U' in there, right?" he continued.

I wrapped my hands around Walter's bicep as he wrote the "U" *after* the "C," adding an "O" and an "S" to finish his handi-work.

"*F-O-C-U-S!*" he shouted to the class. "You've got to *focus* if you want your business to be successful — that's the key!"

My hands dropped as the class erupted with laughter. I smiled in relief.

That was an anecdote I wanted to share (but didn't) at Walter's funeral, held the day after I visited Marcus in the hospital. It captured his often humorous and unconventional style. He had been on my board at NFTE Greater Washington DC for the last three years of his life. I felt humbled that I had been asked to speak about my memories of this remarkable man. Walter had built a very successful company, Convenience Services International (CSI). Two of his products were ServiBar and ServiSafe, the mini-refrigerators and safes installed in hotel rooms. Walter loved being an entrepreneur, and he was also a great family man, with two beautiful daughters and a wonderful wife, Marguerite (who became a close friend). They lived right across the street from my dad's old house on Volta Place, in Georgetown, where I spent several days a week until I was 11, across from the park and the public swimming pool.

At the age of 46, Walter was diagnosed with a brain tumor. He sold the U.S. rights to his business first, and then those in

Latin America as well. In the midst of this crisis, "Wally" decided to volunteer as a teacher at Bell Multicultural High School, in the Columbia Heights neighborhood of DC, and became an adjunct professor at Georgetown, teaching entrepreneurship. Walter was the first person I invited to be a member of the NFTE Washington board, in July of 1995.

"A BizBag? What the hell is a BizBag — that is so *dumb!*" Walter said to me as he sat in the front seat of my Honda Civic after one meeting. I could see in the mirror that one of my colleagues was cringing in the back seat. "Why don't you just get a paper bag — put the NFTE books and a few pencils in it and hand it out to the kids?" Walter and I debated this for the next ten minutes.

"Maybe having a soft-briefcase kit for a young entrepreneur could be a new status symbol," I said, pointing out how Air Jordan sneakers had become status symbols in many communities. "They can also keep their pens, pencils, workbook, business plan template book and NFTE curriculum in one place and hopefully not lose anything."

"Don't kids already have knapsacks?" he asked.

"But isn't it also good marketing visibility for NFTE?" I countered. "Other kids will ask, 'Man, where'd you get that bag? What's that logo mean on the front? Can I get one and start my own business too?'"

Walter got out of the car, mumbling that I had a point but he still thought the bags were b-s. The next week, however, he was standing on the corner of 14th Street and Pennsylvania Avenue directing pedestrians to walk up to Freedom Plaza and meet the

40 NFTE entrepreneurs showcasing their companies.

"These young people are all DC public school kids and young entrepreneurs," he said, handing out flyers. "We need to support them; they are making their first sales."

Many of Walter's Georgetown University students would come to his house — a few blocks from campus — to work on their business plans with him. He didn't like conventional business meetings, so the get-togethers were often in his kitchen. After he died, several of Walter's students called me and shared that, over coffee, he would often ask them: "What are you going to do to help NFTE and inner-city kids learn about business?" When we moved our headquarters, a year later, the kitchen was officially named "The Benson Café," in Wally's honor.

There were many people meeting and greeting and talking together outside the church — sharing their stories about Walter. I saw Steve Mariotti get out of a cab. He had come down from New York. I remembered how Steve had encouraged me to invite Walter to join my board when I was taking over NFTE Washington.

The church was jam packed. I noticed two elegant Latin American gentlemen with "ServiBar" pins on their lapels. One of Walter's daughters gave a particularly moving eulogy, recalling their time living in Mexico on the edge of a forest. Wanting to share a side of Walter that many people there were not familiar with, I talked about how much he meant to NFTE and how he had inspired me personally. After I spoke, it hit me — we still needed him. He cared deeply about this entrepreneurial mission and always made sure I did my best, and now he was gone.

When Steve and I got back to the NFTE office on 15th Street, we were so saddened we could barely speak. Neither of us had been to many funerals and we were both hit by the magnitude of how final it all seemed. I sat at my desk, staring blankly at my computer screen. I was glad I had cancelled my lunch date, I was too depressed. If Steve hadn't been there, I would have just gone home and went to bed.

Even though he was gone, Walter's legacy continued to impact NFTE's mission. In lieu of sending flowers, Marguerite had asked people to donate to NFTE Washington, and the checks had poured in — more than $20,000. But it felt bittersweet to receive this money, because Walter and I had a clear understanding that he would not be giving cash — he would furnish his time (which of course was much more valuable).

In Spring of 2006 we will hold our 8th Walter Benson Youth Entrepreneurship Summit at Georgetown University. Several of his former students contacted us to ask if they could volunteer with NFTE. Two in particular, Rob Coppedge and Chris Caudill, organized a remarkable "day of learning" for a group of NFTE kids at Georgetown, including lunch where the Hoyas basketball team eats, several successful entrepreneurs as guest speakers (mostly Georgetown alums) and tickets to a basketball game. One student attendee, Donald Despratt, was so inspired by the experience that he applied to and was accepted by Georgetown, where he is majoring in accounting and finance. Daryn Dodson, the student who was part of Walter's "F-O-C-U-S" session at BizCamp, started selling ice water on hot summer days, and went on to build three businesses, with a lot of guidance from Walter, over the next several years. As of 2006, Daryn is in his first year at Stanford, studying for an MBA.

After the second Walter Benson Summit, in 1999, Georgetown professor Elaine Romanelli and I met for lunch at Café Milano, to formalize a way for her to get involved. Elaine is a brilliant strategist, a key professor and at the hub of entrepreneurship at Georgetown. She was very close to Walter. I made a number of suggestions and she took to the idea of creating a "NFTE University" teacher-training program at the university, modeled after NFTE's relationship with Babson College. By training 40 to 50 teachers a year, who each in turn went back to their respective schools and taught 50 to 100 kids, Elaine helped build a leveraged model that has helped NFTE "go to scale."

Over the years, dozens of other members from the Georgetown University community have stepped up, including several deans. The program has also been generously sponsored by several local venture capital firms and area foundations. More than 300 teachers have been trained at NFTE U. hosted by Georgetown, who then served more than 22,000 young people in Washington, Baltimore, Delaware, New England, Ireland, the Philippines, and other locations around the world. I have a feeling that Walter would smile if I could tell him that, partly because of his efforts and legacy, NFTE has more kids than we can possibly hand out BizBags to!

* * *

A few hours after Walter's funeral, the buzzer sounded at the office door, and a young and very handsome man came in with a business card and a book in hand. It was Marc, the victim of my two consecutive cancelled luncheon dates that week. I had first noticed him two weeks earlier, while we were both in our cars in adjacent lanes, stuck in traffic near the White House due to a bomb scare. He had actually invited me out to dinner from his car, and I accepted.

I wasn't sure if we had completely hit it off on that first date. Perhaps he was a bit too "New York" (codeword for persistent). He asked a lot of questions and none of his jokes made sense to me. "Julie, he was interviewing you for his mother," said my assistant the next day. "My mother says New Yorkers come on strong."

The twice-cancelled lunch was to be our second date. Marc had come to the office to bring me a book we had discussed at dinner, *Diamonds of the Night* (about the Holocaust), by Czech writer Arnost Lustig, one of Marc's favorite professors from American University.

Steve Mariotti came out to the reception area and I introduced them. "I like him," Steve said, after Marc left. "He's funny. You should give him a chance." Two years later, Steve was one of the 150 guests at our wedding that was held at the ANA (now the Fairmont) Hotel in downtown Washington.

When I first saw Marc, I had thought he was Italian, but it turned out that he was Jewish. My grandfather survived the Holocaust, but I was not raised Jewish. In fact, we celebrated Christmas and I often went with my mother and stepfather to the beautiful Grace Church, the old Episcopalian church in Georgetown. Meeting and falling in love with Marc gave me a connection to my roots, something that had always been missing but which I could never identify. His mother was a cantor (yes, Cantor Kantor, and she sings like a Broadway star and is my number one favorite karaoke buddy) and his father was president of their synagogue on Long Island.

On the day of my wedding, my father was very moody. When we had a few minutes to ourselves, I asked him what was up. "I am a little sad," he said. "You and Tony and Andrew [my brothers] are the only blood relatives that are here. When I was little, there were albums of weddings and births and celebrations in

Hungary — I remember looking through them — but those people are all gone now." With the exception of a very few, much of his family had been killed in the war or had died since.

My dad told me he was really jet-lagged and might not make it past nine p.m., and so we should probably do the father-daughter dance early. But something at the wedding must have changed his mood because he was still there at 11:20 p.m., looking strikingly handsome in a tuxedo he hadn't worn for 18 years, when he and I danced he sang the words to "Sunrise, Sunset" from *Fiddler on the Roof*, along with the band, loudly in my ear.

I believe he was the last person to leave.

* * *

LESSON LEARNED

You need mentors in life. Find someone whom you admire that has made it in business and in balancing work and family, someone you would like to emulate and from whom you could learn. Schedule meetings with this individual — outline how often you will meet or talk on the phone — share your accomplishments and hurdles and ask for concrete advice, questions like: How can I increase my revenues from $100,000 to $120,000 this year? How do I handle my top customer, who is mad at me for shipping an order late? Then you need to listen. Let your mentor know how appreciative you are and how much the advice and support mean to you.

CHAPTER 9

Tom Brown's Story

One in nine families in Washington, D.C., lives on income of $125,000 or more, while one in five lives on income of under $15,000.
— U.S. Census, 2000

On May 7, 1995, Tom Brown stood on the side of the road halfway across the 14th Street Bridge, preparing to jump into the Potomac River and end his life.

"I thought my life had no value," he was telling more than 150 MCI employees some ten years after this near-tragic, transformative event. "I owed some people money and they kidnapped me at gunpoint and took me to Philadelphia, where they finally let me go. By all accounts and the 'statistics' out there, I should be dead, selling drugs, or in prison."

It seemed hard to believe this story, being told as it was by an extremely fit, six-foot-four-inch African-American man in his early forties, who spoke easily, but with a self-deprecating manner that belied his self-confidence. As Tom liked to point out, people sometimes confused him with his "twin," Denzel Washington. But I already knew that what he was now sharing with the MCI staff as part of their Diversity Lecture Series was true.

"I had a favorite uncle who was like a father figure to me, and he had taken his own life," Tom continued. "I thought at the time that I would follow in his footsteps.

"Maybe you remember hearing this on the traffic report. Police cars came to the scene, a helicopter was overhead and police boats waited underneath the bridge. Traffic was at a standstill. Finally, a police officer approached me and said, 'Don't do it man, God isn't done with you yet.'

"I stopped thinking about jumping and started thinking about what he had just said. I realized that I wanted to live. I decided that it would be my life's calling to bring hope to the kids of Anacostia who felt hopeless, like I did.

"I didn't start out that way. When I was 12, I used to sell shrimp to people in Southeast Washington. I loved being an entrepreneur. But as a teenager I was swept up by the streets of Anacostia and got involved in the illegal drug trade. Many of my old friends are now dead or in jail."

Tom went on to share how he got out of Southeast DC and joined the Air Force. After his time in the service, Tom returned to Washington and landed a corporate job. He went on to launch a few start-ups that failed, and then went through a turbulent divorce that led to raising his kids as single father. In 2001, Tom went through our NFTE University teacher certification training program and quickly rose to the top — with his insight, passion, and the business plan he put together with a group of three other public school educators.

In 2004, some of Tom's students from Anacostia High School had participated in a NFTE Youth Trade Showcase at the Marriott Wardman Hotel, as part of a dinner gala we held for over 600 area executives and educational leaders. They were selling clothing, music CD's, jewelry, belts, and catering services. Tom spoke at this event as well and encouraged the audience to meet the kids and exchange business cards.

"You have no idea what it means to them," he said. "A lot of my kids have not spoken face to face with a white person before, or traveled across the Anacostia River. They need to see that they are not 'liabilities' — as they have been labeled by some — but in fact valuable 'assets' to our society and our city's future. For you, it might just be a leather belt or a wallet that a student is selling. For these kids, it might just mean an increase in self-esteem that lasts the rest of their lives."

Tom had started with an after-school program for 15 youths using the NFTE model at Anacostia High. Anacostia, where about only 30% of the students go on to college (and most drop out), is known as the roughest school in Washington. The program caught the attention of a caring principal, who hired Tom part time and had him teaching 86 students. We received a purchase order for $8,400 worth of NFTE BizBags, which the school never paid for, but Tom launched something of great value in a community that desperately needed it.

Tom's words affected the crowd at the dinner gala to such an extent that he was asked by Mike Glosserman, of JBG Properties, what he would need to grow his program. Mike then sponsored Tom's class under the NFTE Adopt-a-Class initiative. Mike personally visited the kids at Anacostia, and they took the Metro to his office uptown in Friendship Heights for sales lessons, business planning, and more. For many of these children it was their first time leaving Southeast Washington, let alone sitting in plush leather chairs in a modern office building. While visiting one day, I saw that 18 of Tom's students were showcasing their businesses in JBG's lobby.

Mike raised more than $37,500 for Tom's several classes. There were bumps along the way, as Tom went from 15 to 120 students enrolled under his "part-time" teaching status at Anacostia, but the program finally got traction. Several students made it to the region-wide business plan competitions. At one, Quinzzy, a young man in foster care, built a wash-and-fold laundry delivery service that took second place. At Quinzzy's graduation, NFTE board member Steve Hall — president of several used car dealerships — showed up at the school with a van on which he had had the name of Quinzzy's business, Four Seasons Wash and Fold, painted on its side. Steve had removed the back seats so there would be plenty of room for Quinzzy to carry the laundry. Quinzzy ended up staying with Tom until he went off to college, and will graduate from Johnson C. Smith University in December 2006, as a double major in Business and Communications.

On one occasion I saw Tom talking on a cell phone in a parking lot, coaching a friend about how to convince her boyfriend not to commit suicide. I've witnessed him talk two boys out of selling drugs and into starting a recording studio, where they created rap music with a positive message. I am convinced that if we could somehow get Tom's message to a broader audience — such as an appearance on *Oprah* — we could reach so many more kids and make an even bigger difference.

In August of 2004, Tom brought Anacostia's new principal to our "NFTE U" training at Georgetown University. We had met with leaders from the Harvard School of Education, who had selected Anacostia High School to be one of the four schools they were going to examine to measure NFTE's impact.[4] Tom's principal pledged his strong support. Last year, Tom had three classes with 65 students in NFTE programs. We sent him a check for $3,250 as seed capital for his students, plus funds for chartering a bus to take them to New York so each could buy $50 worth of goods to resell (this hands-on "lesson" of buying, reselling for a profit, and keeping records is a fundamental experience in the NFTE program).

The week before the trip, Tom was laid off, along with 12 other teachers. Elective teachers are often the first to go when money is tight.

When Tom left Anacostia, it was as heartbreaking to those 65 kids as it was to him. At NFTE, we were distraught, yet powerless to get Tom back his job. However, he told me that it was a blessing in disguise, because he was ready to move on and run his own organization, "Training Grounds." Today, Tom is a youth worker, teacher, minister, father, coach, and has a beautiful fiancée, Kim. We often get together to look at where and how we will collaborate, but the infrastructure and resources needed for starting his nonprofit organization takes time, energy, and discipline. Though we had trained other teachers from Anacostia High School in the past, Tom was the first to achieve breakthroughs there. I often wonder who will keep the torch lit in his place.

---

4 In addition to the finding that, in Boston, NFTE students had a significant increase in desire to go to college, they also felt more connected to school, had an increased "locus of control" and increased independent reading scores — all as compared with a control group

A woman approached Tom at the end of his speech at MCI. She was visibly shaken. "I was there on that bridge ten years ago," she said. "I am so glad you are alive and thriving today. You give me faith for our kids. God bless you."

Tom gives me faith, too. I am proud to call him my friend.

* * *

LESSON LEARNED

We all have our deep and personal reasons for doing the work we do. Understand the personal mission of each member of your team and work every day to coach him or her toward achieving success. For greater sustainability of a high-quality program, youth entrepreneurship needs to be a foundation course, in America's Public Schools and in academies. This will lead to stronger teacher activation and retention. You can have a great curriculum, but you will need a great teacher to bring it to life!

CHAPTER 10

They All Rise Up, With Teacher Mena Lofland

My kids now can see the playing field and they now know how the great game of business is being played.
— Mena Lofland

Last April I flew to New York for NFTE National's annual "Salute to the Entrepreneurial Spirit" awards dinner. This year's gala hap-pened to take place a week before our equivalent "Dare 2 Dream" event at NFTE-GW. Among the impressive VIP speakers, teachers, and young entrepreneurs being honored were NFTE's first honorees from China!

I stopped in New York's wholesale district to replenish supplies of the beautiful stone jewelry that I wanted to buy for three friend's businesses. In particular I bought for a woman who had a new baby and was leaving a high-powered position with a placement agency to build a Mary Kay Business full time. I thought selling jewelry could complement her product line of makeup (she is now a director there).

Then, suitcase and all, I went to the ESPN Zone restaurant, in Times Square, and what a sight to see. About 20 of the young people who would be recognized as Young Entrepreneurs of the

Year that evening, along with their parents, many Teachers of the Year, and some of the organization's key supporters — were all seated together. "You're here for the NFTE party?" the hostess asked. "Yes, I am," I answered proudly. As I walked over, Steve Mariotti had just finished speaking to the group and was introducing Dwight Anderson, one of the adult honorees who was going to be recognized for his support of youth entrepreneurship. Steve waved at me when I came in. It was a very warm moment — here we all were, celebrating NFTE's most promising graduates from all over the world (more than 20,000 young people take NFTE courses annually).

Standing in line for the buffet, I had the chance to talk to a woman I had wanted very much to speak with — behind her, were Bernie Goldhirsh's son and daughter, who had just announced a million-dollar grant for NFTE to expand its programs to Israel, in their father's memory.

"So, Ms. Williams, I'm delighted to finally meet you. Can you tell me your version of the 'house' story?" Her sons, Anthony and Jabious, had just completed a NFTE Greater Washington program and they were being recognized here on a national stage. They had started a business under the coaching of Mena Lofland, at Suitland High School, in Maryland — called SAJA (Same as Jesus Almighty) — the name of their company alluding to being positive role models for other youths.

SAJA is a business that started a few years ago and was expanded in the NFTE classroom. They learned financial management and how to increase channels of distribution. They made over $23,000, and through this revenue they were able to help out their single mom. On January 17th of 2005, Anthony and Jabious presented a 19-page PowerPoint business plan to 12 judges at Allied Capital in Washington, and shared their growth plan. They had four other students with them modeling their fashion line. By that time, they had sold over 2,000 custom-made shirts at church events and elsewhere in their community.

"I am so proud of them," said Ms. Williams. They said to me, "Mom we want to help you get a home — you work so hard." And they gave her several thousand dollars from their first revenues so she could put a down payment on her first home. Ms. Williams, who was just a year or two older than me and worked as a bus driver in Prince Georges County, got quite a Mother's Day present. The glow in her eyes and beautiful smile is a very warm memory.

The next night Anthony stood up at the podium and shared their story (of which we are quoting excerpts):

In 2003, Jabious and I attended Friendly High School. The whole school knew who we were because of our unique clothing designs and uplifting message. But people didn't know that we were going through financial issues. At the same time, our mother had no man to help her or take care of us. We didn't even get our child support checks, and if they did come in my mother needed them for her bills.

We never had a father to give us anything in life, we always got it on our own by doing something positive, such as keeping good grades, and my mother gave us money. My mother kept us in church, and being there taught us how to stay on the right track. We have a lot of younger kids that look up to us as role models and by us staying positive that can help the younger children grow up and be just as positive as they see us. When our mother made a choice to move out of our apartment in Fort Washington, to move to Northeast with my aunt in a small apartment, we thought she was crazy.

We wondered how we were going to design our T-shirts and where are they going to dry? There was already ten people living in the small apartment plus an additional four of us, including my oldest brother, space was very little. Our mother told us that she was making this sacrifice to save money for a house and my aunt was letting us live there for free. It was very hard to make shirts and have a place to sleep. We stayed up late designing shirts for different companies and organizations as well as individuals. When we were in school, we had to get all of our work done and remain with good grades to keep our reputation. We drove 55 minutes Monday-Friday back and forth to school.

Despite all of the confusion and frustrations, we still managed to continue on with the business because of our motive and determination to help our mother. Our principal allowed our shirts to be in the showcases in the school hallways, but some of the students that made fun of our clothing line stole them and wore them to school. We stopped selling in school and just designed shirts and stored them in boxes.

After we produced about 600 shirts, we placed them in our church book store because our pastor knew about our business and had purchased shirts for himself. He

also allowed us to make 600 shirts for the different or-
ganizations. With all of the money that we made from
selling our T-shirts to different organizations, we have
given all of our profits to our mother so she can put a
down payment on our own house and finish paying some
of her bills. One thing we didn't do was keeping a track
of records. But by taking an entrepreneur class at
Suitland with Ms. Lofland taught us a lot. Taught us
how to organize our business and make it better than
ever before.

Ms. Williams was beaming with pride as her sons walked up to the stage in the Marriott Marquis ballroom, in front of an audience of 1400, to receive their awards as Young Entrepreneurs of the Year. Verice White, our Program Director was also at the Marriott Marquis at that table with several board members, myself, and Mena Lofland. "Those are our kids from DC!" they said, when the brothers walked to the stage — we were all hugging and cheering (we were a very loud group).

Mena taught at Cardozo High School in the District for over 30 years, but got tired of the bureaucracy. She did not have full support from her principal to teach the NFTE program there but, based on the results in her students' lives, Mena knew she was pushing the right envelope. In 2002, she had moved on to Suitland High School and her program grew from one class to six in only two years, serving over 160 young people annually.

* * *

Back in 1997, Mena told me about Elisa, a young woman in her class at Cardozo who had dropped out of school. Elisa stopped coming to class and Mena called to ask her to return her NFTE BizBag so some other student could use it. "But Ms. Lofland, I am using it," Elisa said. "If you are not going to come to school, you will need to return it," Mena explained.

So the next day Elisa showed up and slammed the BizBag angrily down on Mena's desk. Mena then got her talking. It turned out that her father had just died and her mother had passed away nine months earlier. Elisa had to move in with her younger sister in her grandmother's house and she didn't want to live with her grandmother. She explained that the books in the BizBag were helping her build a plan to be financially independent, so she was very hurt that Mena wanted everything back.

Mena encouraged Elisa to come back to school, which she eventually did, and ended up doing well in the NFTE program, along with her good friend Melissa, who had also dropped out of school. I met Elisa through Mena and started mentoring both of them on their business plans. One day the three of us sat in a Chinese restaurant on Wisconsin Avenue and discussed Return on Investment. They had dropped out of school again but were only months away from graduation. Melissa, who was 20, had already been kicked out of a school once, but returned to Cardozo so she could graduate. "Why give up now, so soon, so close to graduation?" I asked. We discussed the economics of dropping out of high school in terms of work opportunities, income potential and future life goals. Then we talked about a strategy for making up the schoolwork and negotiating with the teachers to get passing grades, based on improved attitude and attendance.

Two months later I received an invitation from Elisa in the mail to attend her graduation from Cardozo. There she was on the stage, reading Maya Angelou's "Still I rise" poem, and there

was Melissa in the front row, having also graduated that day —
both thanks to Mena's dedication.

Unique among our teachers, Mena has been a NFTE National Teacher of the Year *twice*. She is a no-nonsense individual
who wants her kids to get an edge — and she is coupled with the
"Dream Team" — two NFTE Board members, Patty Alper and
Phil McNeill — who have given their time and energy and financial resources to working with Mena and her students weekly
(Patty is an ace in marketing, and Phil was the Managing Director of Allied Capital). Mena is becoming a legend in our field
and a "big sister" to all the other teachers she comes in contact
with.

* * *

LESSON LEARNED

*There is an old adage, "Shoot for the moon and, even
if you miss, you will always be among the stars".
This saying does not work for Mena and some of the
great entrepreneurs I have worked with. They go for
the moon, period. Time and time again, Mena and
her students have gone the extra mile and "hit the
moon." It can be done if you believe in yourself and
what you are doing.*

CHAPTER 11

Off To Calcutta

We never know how far reaching something we may think, say or do today will affect the lives of millions tomorrow. It is better to light one candle than to curse the darkness.
— B.J. Palmer

Imagine that you have a high school and a college degree — perhaps even an MBA — but there are no jobs for you. One day there is a posting for 300 job openings with the Army. You have no other opportunities and you have children to feed, so you decide to apply. Unfortunately, so do 200,000 others. Rioting breaks out in the fierce competition to get in for an interview. Army officers shoot into the crowd. Three young men are killed.

This actually happened not so long ago in Jaipur, India, a city with an unemployment rate of nearly twenty percent, despite many highly educated residents. There are literally generations of people who walk around aimlessly, with no income for food, medical expenses, or other basic needs. Of the three billion children in the world, 60% live in impoverished areas of Asia and

Africa, according to the World Bank, and the numbers are on the rise.

Jaipur is the hometown of International consultant Harsh Bhargava, who now resides between New Jersey and Virginia. Harsh met Steve Mariotti at a Harvard alumni event in New York. After Steve told him about founding NFTE and his vision, Harsh reflected that if there are no jobs, people needed to be able to create their own livelihoods — as entrepreneurs do. After meeting Steve, Harsh, with his lovely wife Aruna, decided to dedicate themselves to bringing the NFTE program to India. Through their foundation, I Create, Harsh and Aruna raised the funding for a NFTE "train the trainers" five-day workshop in India. They had wanted to hold the training in Jaipur, but their first donor, an innovative New York-based entrepreneur named P.C. Chatterjee, asked that the training be conducted in his hometown of Calcutta (Kolkata), in West Bengal.

In the fall of 1999, four years after I had returned to Washington, Mike Caslin shared Harsh and Aruna's story during a teleconference and announced that we had a grant to hold a teacher training in India for 47 applicants. On a whim, and because I am a NFTE CETI (Certified Entrepreneurship Teaching Instructor) with a travel bug, I tossed my hat in the ring to go to India. Mike called an hour later and asked me to pull out my calendar. I was going to conduct the first "NFTE University" in India and work on a team with Harsh and Aruna!

After carefully weighing the health and safety risks of the trip (neither Marc nor I had ever traveled so far before), it was decided that Marc would join me for a week of sightseeing before the training. Harsh and Aruna were delighted, and helped us plan a six-day tour to Delhi, Agra, Jaipur, and Udaipur. Then

Marc would return home and I would go on to Calcutta.

The beauty, poverty, and spirituality of India floored us both: sensual saris; raw-silk pashmina scarves and shawls; the intense conversations about love, marriage, and American life that we had with people there; monkeys chasing us so we would throw them a snack. One night, Marc and I sat on the veranda at the Jai Mahal Palace Hotel in Jaipur. The scent of the Indian spices and delicacies were intoxicating. I wore a pretty floral dress and felt the warm breeze and the vibrations of the Indian music in my fingers. It seemed as if I had been magically transported to the Oz of my dreams — with the food, wine, the talk, and Marc's beautiful hazel eyes. Elephants came out in the field behind the hotel. They were painted and sparkling with beaded blankets, and the men riding them wore white turbans. Now it was time for the evening polo match: men with long sticks riding elephants and hitting soccer balls! Marc and I smiled at each other, enjoying a second honeymoon just a few months after our first.

Two of the best young entrepreneurs I have ever met were a grade-school-age brother-and-sister team, who sold us beautiful Indian dolls dressed in saris as we were riding an elephant to the top of Jaipur Fort. They actually threw the dolls up to us for selection, and we would throw them back until we found the ones we wanted. We thought 50 cents each was not enough for dolls that would sell at home for ten or fifteen dollars, so we paid a little extra. Marc was treated like a movie star, and people kept asking us about President Clinton's recent visit, and whether we knew him personally.

We traveled by road (instead of by train) so we could really see the country. In Delhi there were monkeys everywhere. We saw cars driving by with three or four people sitting on top of the roof, and buses on the highway with eight or more on the outside of the vehicle holding on by the windows. In the midst of the daily bedlam of cars, camels, bikes, and motor scooters, with everyone beeping to move forward in six or seven different directions, I saw a little naked boy, who looked no older than three, standing alone in the street. While stopped at a traffic light, a woman startled me by knocking on the window. Our eyes meet momentarily. Baby in hand, she looked at me intensely, lifting her hand to her lips in a communication of hunger. I gave her some rupees and our guide admonished me.

Our last stop was Udaipur, where we stayed two or three nights at the Lake Palace Hotel — site of the James Bond movie, *Octopussy*. It was a sparkling white palace in the middle of a lake, and could only be reached by boat. At breakfast the first morning, I sat looking out at the yellow fortresses and the boats with red-and-gold sails, while eating soft bread dipped in honey and drinking strong coffee. On the ride to Udaipur, our guide was fascinated that Marc and I chose each other — a "love marriage," he called it. He had not met his wife until their wedding day, as he trusted his family to find him a suitable mate. He had had the chance to meet her prior to the wedding but, due to his intense respect for his parents, he had opted not to. He said he and his wife have been happily married for 15 years and have three children.

One day, we stopped by a pashmina factory and our guide was with us, but the driver wasn't. I tried to buy six pashminas for women in my family, but the factory owner wouldn't budge from $70 apiece, and I wanted them for $50 — a volume discount. We were in gridlock at $65, so I said I would "pass" for now. When our driver returned, he heard from the guide what had happened. Furious, he asked me to go back to the store. He pulled the owner aside and within two minutes the price was $55. I later discovered that our driver would return for his commission despite the fact that it was a 12-hour drive from his home.

Walking into town alone, we were followed by about 15 people asking us questions and wanting to take us on tours. We were going back to the government shops to find some gifts for our families. We found a small store that made raw-silk clothing and men's shirts. They measured us and within 24 hours we were trying on red-and-blue raw silk with sari material lining the neck and the bottom of the dresses, and men's business shirts, which, after several trips for alterations, were delivered by boat, for less than $30 each!

On the evening of the Festival of Lights, we sat on top of the Lake Palace, camera in hand. We were told that hundreds of women would come down to the water that night and send a candle on a piece of wood out to sea, so that they might get their husbands back in the next life.

I was really nervous about seeing Calcutta. The only impression I had was from the movie *City of Joy*, and I was afraid that I would see much worse poverty than I had already witnessed. On our trip we had already seen tens of thousands of people living in huts with garbage and plastic bags for shelter. Some lived in houses made of cow dung. Marc was heading back home soon, and I wondered what I was in for.

* * *

When I arrived in Calcutta, a new guide picked me up to take me to the hotel where I would meet Harsh and Aruna. The city traffic was much more organized than in Delhi or Jaipur. The large, marble government buildings were quite beautiful. Harsh and Aruna introduced me to Bengali food and music at the hotel restaurant, and we prepared for starting NFTE University in partnership with the I Create Foundation.

People traveled two to four days by train to attend this first training. The big challenge we had was that the Communist Party had led Calcutta and the state of West Bengal for the previous 20 years. The concept of being an entrepreneur was likened to being a gambler, someone who took unnecessary risks. On the first day of training, when we were reviewing the agenda with the class, a man in the front row was shaking his head from side to side intensely at every word I spoke. (I later learned that he was actually nodding in agreement, but in America it would have indicated a big *no* to everything that was being planned.)

Sitting with Harsh and Aruna at the hotel restaurant after the first day, we reviewed the teacher surveys and realized we had some issues we needed to address on Day 2. "I don't want to hear about Henry Ford, Rockefeller and this so-called 'America Dream,'" one had written. Luckily, they had lined up about ten Indian entrepreneurs to speak during the training and make the focus more local.

The next day Harsh, Aruna, and I introduced a phrase that changed everything — "honorable entrepreneurship: someone who does 'good' and does 'well.' " Honorable entrepreneurs can do *well* financially, create jobs for others, and through their success do *good* by giving back philanthropically to the community. We pointed to P.C. Chatterjee as an example. He had moved to New York, had a very successful business there and in Calcutta, and was now in a financial position to support trainings such as this one. Smiles broke out around the room. We had finally cracked the Communist propaganda of putting entrepreneurs in a pejorative light. The teachers started to better understand that entrepreneurs are job creators who can help their communities. They took calculated risks and were not all greedy gamblers.

Several of the teachers had Ph.D.'s in economics, so I was surprised at the less than enthusiastic response when we asked them to write and defend a business plan as the culmination of the training. At least a third of the room groaned and one actually shouted, "I have a Ph.D. in economics! Why should I write a business plan? It's a waste of my time!" It seemed many of the people there who had been teaching business for 20 or 30 years had never written a business plan. But they wrote them, and after the first teacher presented his plan, he was glowing. He confided that it was a lot of fun creating it with a PowerPoint template! Every teacher ended up making a presentation.

On my last day, one of our best trainers, Malti, and a group of other teachers, took me to an amusement park. They introduced me to all kinds of Indian sweets and games. I wish I could have spent another few weeks in India. I was smitten!

* * *

LESSON LEARNED

Leverage is powerful. If each teacher trains fifty to a hundred young people and we train, activate and retain hundreds of teachers, tens of thousands of youths in Calcutta, Jaipur, and Orissa — or anywhere else in the world — can be reached. By training the trainer through a comprehensive and intense program, and providing tools and lesson plans, we can reach young people anywhere. Harsh recently told me that, since this first training, 570 more teachers have gone through a NFTE training, and 20,000 young people have taken an "exposure-level" entrepreneurship course. This year 2,000 disadvantaged Indian children and women will go through a more intensive training.

CHAPTER 12

Four Alumni
(A Cat In A Tree)

Life is understood looking backwards
but it must be lived forwards.
— Søren Kierkegaard

The phone rang. It was Denton Malcolm calling from a 7-Eleven payphone. The police were at his home and he was being evicted. He asked me what he should do.

Denton had recently gotten a new job, and his business activity had slowed down considerably over the past year, due to medical reasons. He had fallen behind on his rent, and was now like a cat in a tree, not wanting to be where he was but unsure how to get down.

A colleague and I contacted lawyers and we found that Denton would need at least $5,000 to keep his apartment, otherwise his clothes and other possessions would be put out on the street. We suggested he return to his place with a car to get his belongings. We knew he had some elegant and expensive clothes for his stage act as a reggae performer. But Denton said he had no car; it was repossessed and he owed $15,000 in back payments.

A loan was out of the question, according to our Chief Financial Officer. In past years NFTE had made loans to many students, teachers, and others but did not have the infrastructure to ensure repayment. "We are not a banking institution and this is not a business loan," our CFO told me.

I told Denton I would call our board chair Sid Smith, of the law firm of Kirkpatrick & Lockhart, to see if we could provide him with legal assistance. What should I do? I asked myself. What could we do as a community to help in situations like these? Just help him pack? Let him learn the life lesson about what happens when you are fiscally irresponsible? Was there something else going on here that I didn't know about?

How could Denton have accrued more than $30,000 in debt in just 18 months? After all the talks we had over the past 11 years, what was it that we didn't get across? He was only 28 and could still build the foundation for a good life. He was a survivor — that I knew!

* * *

"Mary, you've been married almost 50 years. Tell us newbies how to do it. How do you make a relationship last?"

Mary Sturdivant, a NFTE teacher at MM Washington High School in DC, and I, were on the train to New York in 1998, where she would be honored as a NFTE Teacher of the Year. I had watched how she and her husband affectionately gave each other a kiss and a wink goodbye, and how he waited until the train departed before leaving the platform. Marc and I were newly engaged at the time and, being always curious about love and marriage, I asked Mary for her secret.

She replied that a week or two of vacation was mandatory for marital bliss. "You need things to look forward too, to keep the equilibrium," she said, noting that many of their friends and family members were divorced.

"In the old days, Julie, when a cat got stuck in a tree, the fire department, the community, everyone would come out, even at night, and stand around the tree to get the cat down. Think of the cat as the husband or wife. Well, nowadays, when a cat gets stuck in a tree, people don't come out anymore; they are too busy with their own lives — even for the other partner in the marriage. Maybe that spouse is stuck in a tree of his or her own. Maybe the other partner is standing at the bottom of the tree saying, 'Well, *you* got yourself up there, now *you* have to get yourself down!'"

In reflecting on Mary's analogy, I realized that the cat often wants to come down but doesn't always know how. I remembered what a former business leader in DC (who was now in jail after an SEC investigation) had once told me: "Julie, every mistake I have made in my life has been because of my ego. When I was married, I was happy. But I blew it."

About two years ago, a family member of mine became addicted to his medication for ADD (attention deficit disorder).

He would go "doctor shopping" to get more and more drugs. We begged, pleaded, cried, got angry and made threats, but nothing worked. He was up in a "tree" and we couldn't get him down. In fact, his tree became more of a tree *house* — equipped with a DVD Player, stereo, mini-refrigerator and more.

Finally, after realizing that he was stealing credit card numbers from us to feed his addiction and buy things, the family intervened. We initially hadn't realized that the problem was a drug "addiction" until a neighbor who happened to be a doctor helped us put two and two together.

"I don't think he is lying to you," she said in a life-defining conversation. "I think he is hiding an addiction to his prescription drugs and is ashamed."

After a family intervention, he readily agreed to go to a 30-day facility in California to get help. Then, after years in a 12-step program, he came down from the tree and put his feet on solid ground again. The doctors told him that he would have lived only another eight or ten years based on the amount of medication he was taking. But now we have our family member back — it seems like a miracle!

From this experience I realized that sometimes people have to fall in order to get back up. I am always amazed by how honest people can be in sharing both their successes and their failures with my students. It's as if failure is a right of passage for a successful entrepreneur. Perhaps it is for life, as well. To quote Confucius, "Success is not in never falling, but in rising every time we fall."

About an hour after Denton's call, another NFTE alumnus showed up at my office. Richard was also once homeless. He used to come by having worn the same clothes for a week or more. His dream was to be an a capella singer — at one NFTE event, he brought four binders of songs he had written and was dressed in a tuxedo.

Richard had arrived for a promised trip to the record store — his birthday had been a month before. I usually bought him a

CD online at Amazon, but this year I suggested we meet and walk over to Borders Books and Music. Robert seemed to be on cloud nine and looked like a well-groomed college student.

This was the first time I could sit down and really see how much Richard had grown during the past year. He asked me about my family, and then updated me on the changes in his life. He was starting his sophomore year at George Mason University after graduating at the two-year Northern Virginia Community College; he had left a destructive living situation and was happily renting an apartment with a friend. He had a job with the Commonwealth of Virginia, ushered at the Patriot Center, and was in the process of launching a graphic design business as well. Richard was also trying to reconcile with his father, who had been laid off from Office Depot, and find his two brothers, who were both homeless. His mother passed away three years before.

"My brother Luis is jealous of my success," Richard said in dismay. "We had a falling out when I started doing better in life."

Over lemonade and a shared brownie, Richard and I discussed his brand new credit card and the dangers of debt with 18-to-20% interest rates. (I urged him to use the card predominately for emergencies and to pay the entire amount each month.) We talked about the value of getting medical benefits through his job and whether his company might help him pay for college. He was more grounded than I had ever seen him and displayed a deep sense of confidence that he could now do well in his life and help others too. Richard had come down from the tree. Seeing him doing so well after my call from Denton restored my faith that Denton would one day do well again, too.

* * *

Jemil had recently moved with his mother to DC from Texas. Underneath his shy exterior, Jemil was a great competitor, making the football team at Wilson High School as the starting quarterback, despite being only 5 foot 11 with a thin frame. He wore his hair in cornrows, and when he smiled his whole face lit up with enthusiasm. Competition brought him out of his shell.

Jemil had to stop playing football because his grades were slipping and he was on academic probation. But he heard about the NFTE program through Valarie Wheeler, one of our best teachers. Jemil was drawn to NFTE because of the business plan competition. If he couldn't compete in football, why not make some money?

Wilson is considered a fairly well-performing school. About 39% of the students are eligible for free lunches, which is on the border of coming under the category of Title 1 and the types of schools NFTE focuses on. My mother had graduated from Wilson and my older brother Tony taught there. The school has an impressive magnet program in international relations and a very approachable principal, Steve Tarason, who after 38 years has not lost his passion for working with youth.

Twice a year (in November and April) we take eight to eleven busloads of students from the DC area to the New York City wholesale district to buy goods to resell. The students come from many schools in the area and on any given bus there will be kids from more than one school. On one of these trips, Jemil brought several cheesecakes he had baked from his mother's recipe. "Cheesecake slices, just one dollar," he would call out on the bus. He had plain, cherry, chocolate chip, coffee, and strawberry cheesecake for sale. Before we arrived in New York, Jemil had sold more than 20 slices.

After selling some watches and other items he had purchased in New York, Jemil was able to invest in his own cheesecake business. He came to visit our office one day and he shared with me how it felt to be making money.

"I feel like a king!" he said. "I have $20 to $30 in my pocket and it feels so good. Before, I would have to walk a few miles to school every day but now I can take a bus."

Jemil told me he was also helping pay for his mother's bus fare to work. "Finally got some money and I have to *share* it!" he pretended to complain.

After giving the judges a taste of his inventory — along with a copy of his business plan and an advertising flyer — Jemil took second place in the competition, which was hosted by Bill Walton, Chairman and CEO of Allied Capital Corporation. He presented his plan for ten minutes using PowerPoint and fielded questions for another five. Despite not being a notably dynamic speaker, Jemil knew his plan and his financials inside out.

"God has blessed me," he said, when he heard he that he received the second place award and $750 to invest in his business.

Jemil's mother later joined us at a cocktail party to celebrate the students' achievements. "I am so proud of him," she repeated over and over. "You know, when we used to live in Texas, I would also make and sell cheesecakes. I am so proud that Jemil is building his own business now and creating his own recipes."

That May (this was 2002), we had a celebration to introduce

our business plan winners to some important local business leaders. More than 450 people would be in attendance at this early morning breakfast event, which was sponsored by Verizon. We asked Jemil if he would represent all of the students and make a speech. He agreed — he really wanted to come and speak, but mentioned that his mother was having some medical problems. Then I received a call from Jemil's teacher a few days before the event, and learned that Jemil's mother had passed away and he was flying to Atlanta to bury her there.

The room at the Marriott Wardman was filled with 45 tables and decorated with the banners of 22 corporate sponsors. Local business celebrities were there, such as Mario Morino of the Morino Institute; *Washington Business Journal* Publisher, Alex Orfinger; Raul Fernandez, who had built and sold a tremendously successful company called Proxicom; Verizon's former President Marie Johns, plus NFTE's national leadership, down from New York. Out of the corner of my eye I saw a young man in a white suit approaching me. To my great surprise, it was Jemil.

"Ms. Julie," Jemil said. "I'd like to speak." "No problem, Jemil. We'd love to have you."

Jemil (who had taken a plane back from Atlanta the night before), shared what it meant to have his own business. He began: "If my mother were here, she'd want me to face forward with courage and be here today, so here I am. I dedicate my efforts and thank her for being the inspiration behind my business. I know she's in a better place." The audience stood and gave Jemil a standing ovation. Several women ran up to the podium to give Jemil a hug and words of encouragement.

A woman in the audience, Pamela McKee, offered Jemil a

paid internship at the Greater Washington Board of Trade. Several NFTE Board members immediately discussed putting a scholarship fund together for him, and he went on to attend Florida A & M University.

* * *

The most attractive display at the 1995 Youth Trade Showcase belonged to a 15-year-old cake seller named Lelani. The showcase was held at Freedom Plaza, across from the White House. Lelani was in Mary Sturdivant's class at MM Washington.

Mary's class had sold Otis Spunk Meyer cookies and rose-a-grams to raise seed capital for their businesses. Their products here at the showcase were stunning: gift baskets with candles, lotions, sponges; newborn baskets in pink, yellow, green and blue containing diapers, bottles, rattles, and a book on infant care; beaded jewelry; home-made cakes, and more.

Draped with African-patterned fabric, cake samples, and business cards and flyers, Lelani's table won the best booth display award. She had a way of encouraging people to her table and was taking orders to deliver cakes. This was the beginning of Classy Productions Catering and Event Planning.

Lelani started meeting with us every other week after she completed the program, and was invited to cater a DC Chamber of Commerce breakfast event for the education committee, which more than 140 people attended. Dressed in a white jacket and chef's hat, Lelani, driven to the location by her uncle, put out a beautiful spread of delicacies. Next came a gathering on a boat that included the mayor of Washington and several members of Congress.

Lelani, who lives in an inner city neighborhood in Northeast Washington, received a $5,000 scholarship for college from NFTE through the David H. Koch Foundation and several other prestigious scholarships, totaling over $26,000, to help pay her way through Johnson & Wales University.

After graduating *summa cum laude* and receiving a one-year internship at Marriott International, Lelani returned to DC in May 2001 to begin her career in hospitality. But, after 9/11, an estimated 80% of the hospitality workers in DC were laid off due to reduced tourism. Lelani instead got a job selling insurance. She hated it.

"I could go and stand in the unemployment lines, but I thought to myself: I have a valuable skilled called Entrepreneurship and that was the day I decided if I am to succeed, it is up to me," She said.

While taking a Microsoft Small Business class, Lelani bumped into Denton Malcolm and they remembered each other from the NFTE Alumni program. Denton and Lelani spoke about a partnership — that was the beginning of Celebrity Style Catering.

Shortly thereafter, both of Lelani's parents became ill. First, her father lost his battle against lung cancer, and then her mother, who is fighting breast cancer, and is surviving. In addition to the stress of caring for her parents, Lelani also had to contend with her older brother fathering three children with his wife and continuing to be involved in destructive activities that, more often than not, left him incarcerated. This really frustrated Lelani, as she often had to pitch in and help with childcare, while caring for her parents.

Today Lelani is operating a new business, Creations Catering, and also works at the Willard InterContinental Hotel (where Martin Luther King wrote his "I Have a Dream" speech) as a Catering Assistant. She is 26 years old, has made investments, and always has a pitch for her business and a card on hand.

"I can see my future," she would say to us at the office. "I made my first hundred, my first thousand. Now I need to keep going and make that million!"

* * *

LESSON LEARNED

Sometimes, you — like the cat — will get stuck up a tree. When this happens, you will need to reflect on how you got there, how to get down, recharge your batteries, and move on. NFTE has been an anchor for many young people, but in the end they have to be the ones to get back to solid ground. Don't be ashamed of failing. What's more important is that you learn the lessons, determine a new game plan and direction, and face life again — proudly. Don't berate yourself — become your own best friend. That relationship with yourself is lifelong. It is golden!

CHAPTER 13

Hitting it Out of the Park:
The Robert Reffkin Story

Remember always that you have not only the right to be an
individual, you have an obligation to be one. You cannot
make any useful contribution in life unless you do this.
— Eleanor Roosevelt

"**M**y name is Robert Reffkin, and it is my honor to open the evening by sharing a bit of my story, to thank you, and to emphasize the importance of the work *you* can do in the areas of diversity and inclusion," said the confident man at the podium with the clear voice of a 40-year-old CEO, though he was actually a great deal younger.

"My father was an African-American who grew up in the segregated South and my mother was an immigrant from Israel. In many ways, I embody the convergence of race, culture, class, and religion that is the legacy of America. Things were difficult in my family when I was younger. I was supposed to be, perhaps even destined to be, a 'throwaway' — of racially mixed ancestry, disowned by my mother's family, abandoned by my father, and raised by a single mother who was struggling financially."

That struggling single mother was now sitting next to me at the Marriott Wardman Hotel, along with a thousand other people, listening to the "voice of conscience speaker" at the Diversity Best Practice and Women's Business Network International Dinner. I could see tears in her eyes, and she nodded to herself at various points in Robert's talk. We held hands, as he continued.

"So what made the difference in my life? Well, in spite of the hard times we experienced, my mother had an idealistic vision of her adopted country. She believed in the American dream of equal opportunity. It was through my mother's belief in that ideal, her resilience and resourcefulness — and because of people like you who believe in the benefits of diversity — that I gained access to an excellent education, outreach programs, mentors, and worlds of opportunity."

"Among my life-changing experiences was the National Foundation for Teaching Entrepreneurship, which, while I was in high school, trained me to develop a very successful DJ business that helped pay for my education. But, more importantly, it gave me the extraordinary confidence and the entrepreneurial belief that anything is possible."

***

I had met Robert about six weeks earlier, when he called me at my office. He said he was a NFTE alumnus who had just moved into the area and that Steve Mariotti had given him my name and number. He asked if we could get together. He sounded a little old to be a NFTE alumnus, but of course I said I'd meet him.

We sat across from each other at Luigi's Italian restaurant, just two blocks from the office. Robert shared his story with me over the next hour and a half. His high school guidance counselor told him that he would never get into Columbia University and that he should not set his sights so high. But Robert had made more than $75,000 from his DJ business, and he believed in himself. So he flew to New York for the interviews, followed up diligently, and was accepted to Columbia "early decision."

Robert was able to attend college through the profits from his business, along with some outside financial aid and several prestigious scholarships. He graduated in just two and a half years. Then, people told him that he'd never make it to an organization like McKinsey and Company, the renowned business consultancy firm. But he was hired by McKinsey, and was their youngest business analyst. He then went on to Columbia Business School and graduated in a year and a half.

Robert rattled all of this off with a combination of pride and humility that inspired me. I thought to myself: This young man is driven, and has the Midas touch.

After graduate school, he went on to be one of the few minority executives in mergers and acquisitions at Lazard Freres, where he launched an internship program for minorities called Sponsor for Educational Opportunity. Robert was then encouraged to apply for a prestigious White House Fellowship, was one of twelve accepted, and was assigned to be a special assistant at the Treasury Department.

I hadn't realized it at first, but we had met before. While at McKinsey in New York, Robert worked on NFTE National's strategic plan. Now I asked him to join the NFTE Washington Board of Advisors to be a voice for the young people we served, and he agreed. On an impulse, I asked him if he would come back to the office with me so I could introduce him to one of my mentors, Edie

Fraser. She runs the iVillage company Diversity Best Practice and is a real mover and shaker. Edie was there, but she had to go to a planning meeting with her employees. After hearing about 20 seconds of Robert's story she said, "Please, Julie and Robert, join us. I want you to share this with my team."

Edie, and Sandy Butler Wyte, opened their conference room doors and their hearts to me and Robert that day. As a result, six weeks later, Robert was now sharing the podium with the president of Eastman Kodak, the chairman of Chevron, the CEO of General Motors, and many other corporate luminaries.

***

"These experiences have inspired me to use the advantages that have come my way to help others," Robert went on. "My father had given up and died poor and homeless. He was like many of the anonymous people we see every day — forgotten and passed over, their problems ignored. I can never see a homeless person, a child in poverty, or a school in disrepair without feeling a sense of responsibility. What if my father had a program like NFTE to support him? These are not someone else's problems. They are our problems. We must and we can work towards solving them together.

"I am just one person but I am here to remind you that your interest, your efforts, and your commitment to diversity and inclusion has a real face and makes a difference. I know that you will continue this great work and I assure you I will be there with you."

Robert stepped off the podium to a hug from Edie. "He is our legacy," she said to the group from the podium. "He is a benchmark for me of a youth who dares to dream; and for his mother, who has this beautiful and loving son who has brightened her world; and for America, as a White House Fellow."

As dinner was being served, Robert was introduced to Major League Baseball Commissioner Bud Selig. We all agreed: Robert had hit it out of the park!

***

LESSON LEARNED

When you meet people, follow up. Write personal notes and thank-you letters. Staying in touch was a key factor in Robert's success. He used his business ability, work ethic, and follow-up skills to make it to college and get his start in the professional world.

CHAPTER 14

An Army Of Volunteers and One Big Sister

*There are eight rungs in charity. The highest is when
you help a man help himself.*
— Moses Maimonides

There was a time when I felt like I was pushing a thousand-pound rock up a hill, and that — like the mythical Sisyphus — if I stopped, it would roll back down over me. That was shortly after I came to DC from Boston. But we kept planting seeds, and they are now blooming. With the mobilization of a small, competent and diverse army of friends and strategically placed volunteers, everything has changed. Each one of us is now bearing a small part of the weight, and the load is much more manageable.

NFTE Greater Washington DC now has 25 volunteer Advisory Board members (seven are on the Executive Leadership Committee) and last year our entire board was both active and contributed to the organization financially. More than 40 local entrepreneurs and venture capitalists have helped us raise funds for our "Dare 2 Dream" dinner gala, which is held each May. In 2006, more than 150 business plan mentors will help kids in classrooms around the region, providing guidance for their economic and educational futures. In addition, area business leaders will give of their valuable time to judge business plan competitions. To make the classroom experience more meaningful, 16 "adopters" regularly visit our classes and invest their time and financial resources.

The Adopt-a-Class program was pioneered by Patty Alper, a volunteer who is in the forefront of building NFTE in Washington. Our friendship started eight years ago, through her radio program *For Love or Money*. She called me at the suggestion of Andrew Sherman, who chaired my board in 1996 and 1997 and served on NFTE's national board as legal counsel for a number of years.

I sent two of my favorite students to speak on Patty's show: Janelle Stubbs and Regina Jackson. They both began taking the NFTE course at age 11 at Hine Junior High School. Regina beaded jewelry in complex, intricate styles with semi-precious stones. Janelle started a stained-glass window design company. Both continued with their businesses through college.

Patty called me the week after the show to tell me that the students had "blown her away" — she was particularly impressed with the fact that Janelle had invested a percentage of her profits in mutual funds, to save for college. "Julie, my family has just started a foundation," she said. "I'd like to get together with you and learn more about NFTE."

We met for lunch at Bethesda Row, near her office. "I have people that I can introduce you to, that will want to help," Patty said, as we walked along Arlington Boulevard. "But I need to know that they will be appropriately followed up with, you know what I mean? You do so much with such a small team."

There was a kind of challenge in her glance, but also a warmth. After some more discussion, Patty decided to provide seed money to 200 students, so that they could each start a small business with inventory purchased at the wholesale district in New York. She requested that each student write her a memo detailing how the funds were used, describing the business started, and explaining what it personally meant. With this check, from the Small-Alper Family Foundation, we were able to expand this opportunity to ten more schools!

Over the next three years, Patty sponsored our students, donating seed capital, shared their letters with many area business leaders, and joined our Board of Advisors. She also worried about me a great deal. She wanted to make sure I was taking care of my health, that I wasn't overdoing it. "I know I am a pain," she would often say to me. "Just tell me to stop if I am going too far." She did demand a lot out of me and my team, but, after our first meeting, I knew that Patty cared very deeply about NFTE's mission. Over time, it became more and more clear that she was helping me take NFTE Greater Washington to a new level.

Once, after looking at our existing Citywide Business Plan Model, Patty decided that seeing students present their business plans using PowerPoint software at downtown locations would be an excellent marketing opportunity to involve more people with NFTE — especially wealthy individuals and corporate leaders. Her foundation funded a sit-down, full-service luncheon for the judges before the competition, which really connected our judges to each other and NFTE. We asked the judges to share how they made their first dollar. Over the dozen or so competitions, Patty and I marveled at some of the answers: breeding pigs, selling hair pomade door-to-door while singing a promotional jingle, hauling trash — along with the more traditional newspaper routes and babysitting.

After the luncheon, Verice White, our program director, introduced our students and their teachers:

"My name is Bruce Proctor. I go to Wilson Senior High School, and the name of my business is Twin Sports. My partner is my brother Glenn."

"My name is Mirada Daniels and the name of my business is Get it Girlz. I go to Lincoln Junior High in Washington, D.C."

"Today we declare our freedom to be entrepreneurs. I am free. I am an entrepreneur," they would recite from the "NFTE Creed."

Patty's suggestion to use our Citywide Business Plan model as NFTE's key donor cultivation expanded the organization significantly. When we asked our board members how and why they got involved with NFTE, at a retreat in 2002, 80% replied that the original impetus had come from being a judge at a business plan competition.

The Adopt-a-Class concept had its origins in an after-school program that Riggs Bank (now PNC) underwrote at Anacostia High School. Riggs brought in executives to help the kids and provided a small stipend for the teacher. One year we asked a student, the teacher (Tom Brown), and the Riggs Executive (Anne Knight) to share their experiences with the program to an audience of more than 400, including Patty. She decided to donate $10,000 to her alma mater, Wilson High. "I want just one class and I want to work with them and fund their experience," she said. "I want to be hands-on and support them in their business plan development."

So we created a budget for $500 per student that included seed capital, BizBags, funds to open bank accounts, BizTech student licenses, a teacher stipend, NFTE management support, field trip transportation, and more. We had now launched our first official Adopt-a-Class program! Patty was delighted to be working with "her" kids, especially Bruce and Glenn Proctor, who won the regional and national contest that year (and are now working on a clothing line for Beyoncé).

In a letter to their school, Bruce and Glenn wrote: "We want to give to others the way Patty and Phil [McNeill, her co-adopter and fellow NFTE Board member] gave to us. Here is our game plan. We are coming back into town in early December and would like to speak to the entrepreneurship class. We would also like to send the school $5,000 for the entrepreneurship program." Patty and Phil started bringing in friends to see the class. Patty resigned from the board to do consulting and create an Adopt-a-Class "cookbook" — a recipe for growth. There were a lot of issues to address: managing teachers, donor expectations, asking top business leaders to walk through metal detectors, student discipline, and financial sustainability, to name just a few.

"Julie, this is so exciting, you just have no idea," she said to me one day while we were sitting in her car in front of the NFTE office. "It's just amazing to see the impact of this program." After a string of meetings, we went on to introduce Adopt-a-Class to Patty's extensive network of contacts, from which there were an increasing number of individuals who were mobilized by her passion and became interested in the program. The program grew from one adopter to three, then nine, and now there are more than 22 adopters in 10 schools — and it continues to grow. Eighty-four percent of the adopters return each year and many recruit new ones.

Patty was attracted to NFTE's mission because it marries business and philanthropy. Before she was in radio, Patty was a partner in an extremely successful construction business. As the head of marketing for the company — her strengths were in sales and customer relations — her love for the entrepreneurial spirit grew over the years.

"These are both important sides of me," Patty remarked to me once. "That's why NFTE works for me — especially when I get letters from the kids, which gives me something real to take back to the foundation. This matters so much more to me than other philanthropic pursuits. I like to see how my money is used and so do the other adopters. People don't just want to write a check, they want to be involved."

Over the next few years I came to realize more and more that she was right. *The New York Times* and *Washington Post* columnist Steve Pearlstein wrote stories about Adopt-a-Class: "My only question is, why isn't NFTE in 30 more schools in the region?"

Patty's program is being talked about all over the country and abroad. It now comprises 17% of our budget in DC, and is so important that I am investing much more of my energies walking into more classes than ever with our adopters and connecting them to the teachers and principals.

* * *

Patty is wonderful — quirky, impeccably dressed, passionate and demanding. She is the closest thing to a big sister I have ever had. Sometimes we sit across from each other at a restaurant or in her car following a meeting and talk for hours — about

NFTE, Adopt-a-Class, how we could refine the model, how we could better encourage NFTE National to take this on, making a movie about NFTE, our childhoods, our mothers, life, music, being a wife, and being Jewish women.

When students from her classes win competitions, she and Phil just beam. "Those are our kids!" she shouted when Twin Sports (sparkling headbands and clothing) or Clarence Cross (the Donut Kid) or Dexter Briscoe (who sells jackets on eBay) or Aquatic Kings (fish tanks and monthly cleaning contracts) won first place in their respective competitions.

Patty has been a big part of NFTE's success in Washington. Ten thousand local young people have completed the NFTE program in the last ten years. In 2005, NFTE Greater Washington DC was rated the top regional office in the entire organization. We trained 2,154 students and raised $980,000 locally. We have built an equity position of more than $500,000, for sustainability. We have been featured recently on CNN, in *The Washington Post*, *Business Week*, *The New York Times*, and other media outlets.

School is meant to prepare a student for life, for a solid economic future. But the typical high school training does not always prepare young people for success in our market economy. NFTE's "mini-MBA" curriculum is sorely needed.

In Washington, D.C., only half of our young people are graduating from high school and of those only 20% are going on to college. The physical condition of some 80% of our schools is listed as "poor," and we have a new Superintendent who is supportive and is making good strides. In many ways, the challenge is greater than ever. We are just starting to climb the mountain.

***

LESSON LEARNED

Build a team of catalytic people who energize others. You can't go it alone. If you are just starting, put together an advisory board who will roll up their sleeves and work with you. Ask them for their help in three areas: time, financial resources, and networking.

CHAPTER 15

Juggling Life: Glass Balls and Rubber Balls

"Julie, here is my advice for you. In life, there are rubber balls and glass balls and you are always juggling. Your family is glass, so you can't drop them. Many of your work projects are rubber balls — the assignment will still be there tomorrow and you need to plan in advance. And sometimes a work project becomes a glass ball, and you have to let your family know you need to put them down for a day or three. Because they know they are 'glass' to you, they are more likely to understand and respect that you have a glass project this week. That's how I've been able to balance work and family."

Those words have stayed with me ever since I heard them, told to me by a man I met at the Price-Babson Fellowship Program in 1994. I attended as an entrepreneurship educator; my corporate partner was Tom Hartocollis of Microsoft, whom I had met earlier that year. It was an amazing week of case studies and lessons in teaching entrepreneurship. Some influential people were there, such as Jeffry Timmons, author of *New Venture Creation*; Jiffy Lube founder Stephen Spinelli; and Bill Bygrave, head of Babson's Arthur M. Blank Center for Entrepreneurship.

But the day this advice really hit home was on September 12, 2001. I was looking in the mirror at the Washington Sports Club, in downtown DC, trying to pull myself together for a board meeting. Even though it was the day after the 9/11 attacks, I hadn't cancelled the meeting because I thought people would need an opportunity to congregate and talk.

I had been in Manhattan the day before, at the NFTE national offices at 120 Wall Street, when I got a call on my cell phone from Marc: "Julie, a plane just hit the World Trade Center!"

"What? Let me turn on the TV."

Everyone ran to the conference room and we turned on the news. I thought Marc had meant a small, private plane — but no, it was a passenger jet. We saw the images of the World Trade Center burning as a second plane came into the picture. We heard a *pop* from outside the window and then the TV shut off. I looked outside over the South Street Seaport to see burning and charred papers billowing down from the sky.

My phone rang again.

"Julie, you have to get out of there — we need you to get out of there," said Marc. "A plane just hit the Pentagon! Go to your Mom's apartment." (My mom lives in the city. My parents were both overseas and neither knew that I was in New York.)

It was not until this moment that I realized it was my 32nd birthday. Everything felt surreal, as if I were living the stories I could only imagine from my Dad's life in Hungary during World War II, with bombs exploding around him.

We agreed to stay put — we had food and shelter, while there was only chaos and perhaps very real threats outside. I looked out the window into a swarm of dust, and it seemed like thousands of people were walking on the street below like a parade of zombies. If I went outside, would it burn my eyes? Was it toxic?

Steve Mariotti called from his apartment in Greenwich Village. "Don't come in, don't come down here," insisted Dave Nelson our COO, who joined NFTE after a very successful 30 years at IBM, and Mike Caslin added, "We're all fine."

In retrospect it was a good idea to stay inside, as the towers would soon be falling. We half talked about business, half about what to do, and every 30 minutes on the radio we'd get another report of more planes "out there and unaccounted for." Suddenly the elevator opened and in walked Steve, brushing the dust off his blazer. He couldn't stand the idea of the team being there without him. "Hey guys," he said with a big smile, "what's the game plan?"

At about 2 p.m., we got ready to evacuate the building. I took one more call from Marc, and my sister-in-law, Zena. When I got to the elevator the staff, led by Mike and Steve, sang "Happy Birthday" to me with the biggest smiles they could muster. But now it was found that the elevators didn't work. Dave, who was recuperating from a broken leg and was on crutches, had to be virtually carried down the 29 flights of stairs. We took some NFTE T-shirts soaked in water so we wouldn't have to breathe the noxious fumes when we got outside.

Mike Caslin found a gurney, wheeled Dave uptown until he found a car that was driving to Connecticut (where Dave lived) and then returned to the wreckage at Ground Zero and assisted in assembling the first morgue. Eventually, he and other civilian volunteers were relieved by the New York State National Guard. (Mike has written about his experience in detail in a powerful book called *Fallen Innocence, Towering Love.*)

It took me six hours on foot to get to my mother's apartment on West 79th Street. Along the way, I was touched by the generosity of New Yorkers. "Do you need to make a call? Can we get you food or water?" they said to people who had been walking from the scene of the disaster. Thank goodness Steve lent me some socks he had in the office so I could change my shoes from heels to flats.

NFTE National closed down for several weeks as the city put emergency plans into effect, which included cutting off access to lower Manhattan. The small businesses, mom-and-pop stores near the office, suffered, and many would never reopen.

I went to Penn Station the morning of the 12th and got on a 5 a.m. train, praying that it wouldn't blow up. I know that sounds melodramatic now, but nothing seemed safe at the time.

* * *

I pulled out the black Ann Taylor dress with white piping and the black pumps that Marc bought me at Union Station that morning before I arrived. The rest of my clothes would stay in a suitcase in a closet at the NFTE New York headquarters for the next four months.

I reached into my knapsack and took out my makeup kit. My brain went whirling again. In just two days, the movers would be taking all our things to a new home in the Palisades section of Northwest DC — our dream house. Would we live until then? Was DC safe or still a target?

Now I could finally listen to my cell phone messages, which I could not retrieve in New York do to the heavy call volume. They ranged from "Happy birthday, Sis! Let's have dinner," to "Oh My God — you're in New York!" to "Julie, we got your message and we are concerned about you all in New York. Just call us," to "Honey, we are in Italy. Happy Birthday! We love you. Going out to lunch and then meeting up with Cici and Angelo. Love you! Mom," to "Honey, call us. We got the news in Italy. Call us!"

I walked from the Sports Club to our NFTE offices. Soon our board members began arriving. We talked and hugged and shared stories and fears. It was so good to see Patty, Phil McNeill, David Roodberg, and everyone else. Seeing them again centered me. We decided that we needed to redouble our efforts and that our kids in DC should be made to feel safe.

There was a time when I thought I should just serve and help people, and that maybe I wasn't going to have my own family — maybe that wasn't my role in life. I worked hard and passionately and I loved what I did. But, that day, I realized that there was nothing more important than family.

Less than two years later, we had Justine Sophia — our own miracle. Up until then, NFTE had been my baby. Now I have joined the ranks of those who try to juggle those glass and rubber balls while building a life and balancing the things that matter most. It's all about family — my family and the extended family at NFTE. We are joined together on this journey.

* * *

Appendices

A Winning Lesson Plan You Can Use:
The Bu$ine$$ Start-up Game

Over the past 14 years, I have personally taught entrepreneurship to over 800 young people and trained more than 350 Certified Entrepreneurship Teachers, who then reached well over 20,000 other youths.

I noticed an ad from the Children's Defense Fund: "Work your body and some day you might play on the team — work your mind and some day you might own the team." There is certainly a lot more room at the top for innovative entrepreneurs than slots for players in the NBA, NFL, and MLB.

Every year I am asked to speak about entrepreneurship in such venues as schools, juvenile detention facilities, and youth organizations. Here is my proven "stealth lesson plan" it takes just 45 minutes to present.

Here's how it goes: I walk into a classroom of 10 or 20, or even more (I have done this with a group of 80), and play the "stand up, sit down" game to get them focused and to make them realize this isn't going to be a "lecture," that it will be interactive.

"How many of you got to bed before 11 o'clock last night? Stand up if the answer is yes."

"How many of you think Denzel Washington is a great actor?"

"How many of you went to the beach this summer?"

"How many of you already own your own business?"

"How many of you would like to own your own business in the future?"

"Good job! Wow. About 60% [I say for example, estimating the percentage by the number standing]. Interesting. Can you tell me about the kind of businesses you'd like to own?" And then I point to individuals and get some responses.

I love hearing the ideas they have. I then find out who is working part time — usually 40% in a group of 14-17 year olds, who will be making from $6.10 (minimum wage) to about $8.00 an hour.

Reaching into my "toolkit," I pull out five pashmina-style scarves, five bottles of perfume oil, five men's watches, five Mont Blanc-style pens, five colorful men's ties, and five makeup cases (containing six eye shadows, six shades of lipstick, and two blushes).

"Okay, let's pretend we're at the Pentagon City Mall [pick a large, popular mall in your area] and we see a booth selling these items, and a lot more besides.

"Start with the pens — what do you think they would cost at the booth? I'll pass them around so you can take a closer look."

One student says: "Five dollars." "Ten," says another, and "Eight," another. Students are now heavily engaged with making their estimations. I take a class average — let's say it's $8; I write that number on the board. Next product: the pashmina scarves — the class average is $12.

We go through all the products and there is disagreement and debate on the prices. ("Nah, I saw those at a flea market for $5; or: "It can't be that much, that's not real silk.")

Here's a hypothetical final table for the prices of this particular group of products:

Product	Selling Price
Pen	$8.00
Pashmina	$12.00
Makeup Case	$8.00
Tie	$10.00
Watch	$22.00

"Okay, now I want you to all close your eyes," I say to the class. "I want you to walk into the Pentagon City Mall and see that *beautiful* booth with all the things we've discussed here and a lot more. It's almost Christmastime and the mall is bustling. At the booth you see a sparking new cash register and on top of it is a baseball cap that has embroidered on it: I AM AN ENTREPRENEUR. I want you to put the cap on — go ahead, try it on. This is *your* business. Now, open your eyes. Look up at the board. We discussed all these prices, but my question for you is, now that *you* own the business, what's a crucial question you will want to know the answer to?"

"Is the quality good?" one student asks.

"Good question. Others?"

"Will people buy these?"

"Excellent."

Then one student looks at me and asks : "Will I make a profit?"

"Excellent! Let me ask you this. If you buy the pashminas at $20 each, would you sell them at $12?"

"*Noooo*," the group answers in unison.

"Why not? " I ask.

"Because you'd lose money," will come the answer.

I share that we take hundreds of students annually to wholesalers in DC and New York City and that I am going to tell them what, in business, should never be revealed: *the wholesale cost* (Cost of Goods Sold: COGS) for these products.

Product	Selling Price	COGS	Gross Profit
Pen	$8.00	$2.50	$5.50
Pashmina	$12.00	$4.00	$8.00
Makeup Case	$8.00	$2.00	$6.00
Tie	$10.00	$3.00	$7.00
Watch	$22.00	$7.00	$15.00

"So, how much would you make if you sold one pen?" "$5.50." "And one pashmina?" "$8.00." "Okay, now this is very important. Most of you that are working said you were making about $7 an hour. *Is there a law in the United States of America* that says you, Deshaun, or you, Michaela, can only sell one pashmina an hour, so you don't make more money than your friend, who is working at McDonald's? " "No," the class answers, mesmerized. I always have their full and undivided attention at this point. Always.

"Could you sell two pashminas an hour? Could you sell four? Might you sell none? Whose hands is it in?" "Mine," the students will say together. "And you will be selling something people want, right? Okay, if you remember only one thing that I said today it is this: If you ever get fired, or if a parent or someone you know loses a job, remember that there are other ways to *provide* for yourself and your family."

I always get nods and a collective "Yes." The lesson ends there — I call it the Business Start-Up Game and it has always been a winner. At this point, I might hand out applications to students who want to attend a NFTE summer BizCamp and learn more about entrepreneurship. Then, if I am teaching an actual full 54-80 hour class, I will take it one step further:

"I'd like each of you come up here, pick a product, and when everyone has done that, I'd like those of you who took the same product get together. Now I want each group to do the following and decide:

What is the name of your company?
What is your product and what consumer need will it fill?
What is the price you will charge?
How will you promote your new business?

Where will you sell it?

They will now be immersed in the concepts of the "Four P's" of marketing — price, product, place, promotion. I have found that young people will come up with terrific ideas for promoting their businesses.

The last piece is, I pull out a receipt book and give each student a receipt and suggest taking the product and selling it. The following week, they should come back with the receipt signed by the customer and with a memo on how the sale went and when they sold the item. Eighty-five percent of my students make that sale within the first 72 hours. Then we discuss the income statement and the fact that there are other costs that they will have to take into consideration, such as: Utilities, Salaries, Advertising, Interest, Insurance, and Rent, plus Depreciation (USAIIRD). Then open our NFTE textbooks to *Chapter 1: What is Entrepreneurship* — and the course proceeds from there.

* * *

Where Are They Today?

Deshaun Houston is married and works as a Campus Police Officer for the Department of Public Recreation in Brockton, Mass. He is also building an Entertainment Business called Ministry Entertainment. Deshaun owns two real estate properties that he purchased at the age of 24, including a three-family home that he rents out. Additionally, he rents out the garage apartment of the single-family home he and his wife currently live in. In speaking to Deshaun, he expressed a desire to see NFTE back in Brockton, and would even consider teaching the program himself.

Rashidi Sheppard was last heard from when he was in the Marines in Okinawa.

We are still trying to find **Jason** (Westside Alternative High School), and **Anton Sanders** (Roxbury Island School).

Kathleen Jeanty graduated from Babson College and is the CEO and President of her public relations firm, InnerLeaf (www.InnerLeaf.com) She is in the process of opening a second office. She is raising her seven year old son as a single mother. In January of 2006 Kathleen's company won a contract to represent NFTE Greater Washington DC's Regionwide Business Plan Competitions.

Jabious Williams received a full scholarship to Southeastern University in Southwest Washington. The entire faculty wore garments from his clothing line on Orientation Day at the school led by social entrepreneur and former city council leader Charlene Drew Jarvis. **Anthony Williams** still runs SAJA Inc. with his brother, and will graduate this year (2006) from Suitland High School. He would like to start an after-school CEO Club for other young entrepreneurs.

Dolly Morales married and has two children. She has a long-term, full-time job with a NFTE Board member in New Bedford and is operating a landscape business with her husband.

Michelle Araujo set up a health-food kiosk business in New Bedford, with her husband and three children. She has obtained a degree in Social Work.

Denton Malcolm moved in with his sister and is working full time at Chipolte Restaurant to build financial security while he expands the offerings of his business development company, D.A.M LLC (damcoworldwide.com).

Mena Lofland, after 39 years, plans to retire from teaching after this semester and operate her own tour guide firm in Washington, D.C. Steve Pearlstein's column on the front page of *The Washington Post* Business Section on May 27, 2005 read:

Among Washington area schools, DeMatha comes to mind when thinking about the powerhouse in basketball, Thomas Jefferson for National Merit Scholars. But probably few people, even in Prince George's County, realize that Suitland High has become the regional powerhouse in entrepreneurship... Lofland is one of those dedicated, no-nonsense teachers who comes to class with high expectations and sees her job as preparing her students for a world that isn't interested in sob stories or excuses but rewards hard work and a good idea.

Patty Alper is in the classroom weekly at Suitland High School with Mena and her co-adopter, **Phil McNeill**, mentoring students on their marketing plans and financials, to give them an edge when they graduate and go out into the world. I just learned that Phil is investing in a clothing line business run by two NFTE graduates who went through the program at Wilson High School in 2003.

* * *

Budgeting For Poverty[5]

The federal government says a family of four earning $19,307 or less a year is living in poverty.

How far does $19,307 go in America today?
How do you budget? What do you leave out?
You make the hard choices.

Housing?　In America, a family of four earning $19,307 a year will spend on average $5,329 annually for the most basic of shelter.

$$\begin{array}{r} \$19,307 \\ -\ 5,329 \\ \hline \$13,978 \end{array}$$

Utilities?　To keep a family of four warm and secure, the average expense for utilities and public services runs $2,309 a year.

5This powerful presentation is reprinted with the permission of the Catholic Campaign for Human Development. This document is available as a flash animation tour to help raise awareness about the economics of poverty in the United States. Visit www.povertyusa.org to learn more.

$13,978
$\underline{-\ 2,309}$
$11,669

Transportation? A family at the poverty line will spend $4,920 a year to own and maintain a used car, and fill it with the gas and oil needed to go to work, to day care, to the store, or wherever.

$11,669
$\underline{-\ 4,920}$
$6,749

Food? Even with public assistance such as food stamps, families making $19,307 will spend $4,102 a year for food at home and away.

$6,749
$\underline{-\ 4,102}$
$2,647

Health Care? Even if an employer contributes part of the costs of health insurance, a family of four at the poverty line would still pay on average $2,132 year for health and medical expenses. The cost of not having health insurance, however, would be devastating.

$2,647
− 2,132
$515

Child Care?   The costs in a metropolitan-area child care center for two children five and under can reach over $13,000 a year. Even with child care subsidies, low in come families with two small children will spend on average $2,300 a year on child care.

$515
− 2,300
−$1,785

So now you're $1,785 over budget, and you still don't have everything you need.

What did you leave out?   Toiletries, School Supplies, Shoes, Clothes, Holiday Gifts, Education, Life Insurance, Furnishings, Recreation, Cleaning Supplies, Entertainment, Birthday Gifts, etc.

These are the decisions that people are forced to make every day when they live in a state of poverty.

* * *

VISION FOR NFTE STUDENTS

*That every young person in poverty must learn the
fundamental skills to earn at least $100 a day to
"exit" poverty. Seeking higher education, building a
business, being an 'intrapreneur' or a good employee
candidate are all viable paths for motivated youth to
be economically productive members of society.*

Source of Statistics:
Rent, utilities, transportation, food, health care: *Consumer Expenditures Survey*, U.S. Department of Labor, Bureau of Labor Statistics, June 2005;
Child care: *Expenditures on Children by Families*, United States Department of Agriculture, Center for Nutrition Policy and Promotion, April 2005;
Poverty threshold: U.S. Census Bureau, Income, Poverty, and Health Insurance Coverage in the United States: 2004

Early Testimonials To
I Said Yes!

We hear every day that the future of our communities are in the hands of America's youth. Through NFTE and the kids profiled in *I Said Yes!*, Julie takes the future in her hands and gives kids a chance to build real entrepreneurial skills. What better way to give us hope?

> — *Alex Orfinger, Publisher,*
> *The Washington Business*
> *Journal*

So many people have not walked the walk and therefore can not experience or understand the obstacles and trauma that many young men and women have overcome to not only survive, but to thrive. Thank you, Julie, for walking the walk and for giving us these truly inspirational accounts. The suffering, sweat, tears, loss, grievances, but also the laughter, trust, perseverance, honor and integrity. It allows others to open their eyes to the walk to which you and others at NFTE have so graciously dedicated your careers. It allows others to understand how important your educational opportunities are for so many of our nation's young men and women —opportunities many couldn't have dreamed of. Most importantly, it pledges hope, and inspiration to young men and women who face misfortune or adversity.

> — *Joseph E. Robert, Jr., Chairman*
> *& CEO, J.E. Robert Companies*
> *Chairman, Fight For Children*

Through the formalized teaching of business principles to some of the neediest of America's youths, Julie Kantor's infectious passion about making a difference has opened up a new and exciting world to countless young people who now see entrepreneurship as a turning point in finding their own voice and managing through some of life's toughest challenges. In instilling what seasoned entrepreneurs face daily — how to triumph over failure — students learn the rewards of perseverance, idea-creation, self-esteem, drive, passion, focus and goal-setting, allowing them to envision and achieve their personal dreams in life.

> — *Julia Spicer, Executive Director,*
> *Mid-Atlantic Venture Association*
> *(MAVA)*

The real-life stories in *I Said Yes!* make for a powerful and eye-opening read. It makes us realize that it is imperative that our children receive the academic preparation and community support needed to succeed in life. Our country's educators would benefit from reading these compelling vignettes and applying the lessons learned to their classrooms and schools.

> — *James V. Kimsey Chairman*
> *Emeritus, America Online, Inc.*

Teaching entrepreneurship to urban teens not only changes their understanding of business, it teaches life skills and is a wonderful learning tool. *I Said Yes* is about opening vistas to young people who never dreamed what could be over the horizon for them.

— Charlene Drew Jarvis, President, Southeastern University

The stories in *I Said Yes* are emblematic of the intensity, drive and energy that Julie Kantor has brought to the NFTE program and the youths she has touched with the "magic" of entrepreneurship. Having been directly involved with Julie and her work, I can speak first hand of the impact the sense of entrepreneurship has once it is instilled in these young people. To see the expressions on their faces as they show you their products is truly a memorable experience. In an era where conceptual skills are of great importance, giving young people the encouragement and opportunity to think entrepreneurially serves them, our school systems, and nation well. Whether they build their own business or bring an innovative mind and sense of possibility to other areas of their lives, the benefits are clear.

— Mario Morino Chairman, Venture Philanthropy Partners

I've seen first hand the work of Julie Kantor and NFTE in Greater Washington and know that the stories and experiences contained in *I Said Yes* are a great read for any educator and aspiring leader! Julie is a true social entrepreneur and we're glad that NFTE is a member of the Nonprofit Roundtable and even gladder about its impact in the public schools in and around our Nation's Capital.

> — *Chuck Bean, Executive Director,*
> *The Nonprofit Roundtable of*
> *Greater Washington*

Youth entrepreneurship has reached its "tipping point," and Julie is at the forefront of this incredible movement that is impacting thousands of youths around the world. I have benefited personally from the free enterprise system, and helping youth make it in the market economy is the right cause for me. I have seen the program in action, I have heard youths present their business plans, I have met these young entrepreneurs, and I only wish I had had this program when I was younger.

> — *S. Tien Wong, CEO, Opus8, Inc.*

Your book is superb! You helped launch NFTE-I Create in India with the pioneering "Training the Trainers" workshop in Calcutta in 2000. The term "honorable entrepreneur" that we coined together in Calcutta is still used extensively in all our four centers in India. There's poetry in your writing. The description of your visit to Jaipur and Udaipur transported me into a magical world. So beautifully written, straight from the heart.

> — *Dr. Aruna Bhargava, Author*
> *of "Everyday Entrepreneurs"*
> *and Director Program Develop*
> *ment, NFTE-I Create, India*

I Said Yes Is powerful as entrepreneurship is a powerful and potent force in my life. Trials and tribulations have come into my life like winds and sudden storms, yet I've banished all reasons for failing and grasped all reasons for succeeding. I am an entrepreneur.

> — *NFTE Alumnus, Denton*
> *Malcolm, Chairman and CEO*
> *D.A.M Companies, LLC*

Providing hands-on business experience helps to build great confidence in young people by teaching them to think for themselves. Through programs like NFTE, youth entrepreneurs, guided by real-life business leaders, learn to not only dream big, but how to find the steps to make their dreams a reality. The youths in Julie's program learn at an early age how to pick themselves up if they fall and move forward to success. They are not stopped by challenges or mistakes, but learn to look for the lessons in each situation. This is how real leaders are created; these young people get the chance to do this early and in a way that provides them focus, direction and inspiration.

> — *Tim Kime, President,*
> *Leadership Washington*

"Entrepreneurship needs to be a part of every child's schooling inAmerica and Kantor's book, *I Said Yes*, hits it dead on. In order for our children to succeed in this ever so competitive global economy, youth entrepreneurship must be an integral part of our educational system."

> — *Brien Biondi, Executive*
> *Director, Chief Executives*
> *Organization Former CEO,*
> *Young Entrepreneurs'*
> *Organization*

I am passionate for all to read and share this unique entrepreneurial book, *I Said Yes Real Life Stories of Students, Teachers and Leaders Saying Yes! To Youth Entrepreneurship in America's Schools.* Thanks to the special youth catalyst and author, Julie Kantor, for her caring and compassionate contribution. These youth are our future. Entrepreneurship for our inner city youth is our hope, the dream, the reality of providing real, sustained economic and substantive change. The stories are compelling. The students are energizing. They and their teachers give us hope. Those who say "YES" to a product or service that is needed and apply the business discipline to growing a market share are those who provide inspiration to so many others. These messages are vibrant, Yes, I can do it as a young person! Powerful contribution, Julie Kantor!!!

— Edie Fraser, President, PAG:
Diversity Best Practices, Business
Women's Network and BPCC